How To Keep Him

It's the most complicated, fascinating, delicious emotion of all and, at its best, it makes us feel deliriously happy. I'm talking about love of course. Here at Cosmopolitan we are dedicated to your love life – after all, who doesn't want to be loved – but we also realise that in busy lives full of work, play and sex, love and romance can sometimes be forgotten. That's why we've gathered together the most invaluable love advice you'll ever need. From finding your dream man to recognising and overcoming all the relationship hurdles along the way, think of this as your mini love advisory service – always there when you need it.

This confidence-boosting manual, filled with the most practical, fun and 100% helpful tips, is a must-read. Enjoy every page and never be disappointed in love again. And remember, Cosmopolitan is the only magazine you can trust for all your relationship advice. Write in and let me know what you think.

LORRAINE CANDY
EDITOR-IN-CHIEF

HOW TO

Meet Him

Finding
YOUR DREAM MAN

Finding your Dream Man can be more tedious, dispiriting and frustrating than public transport on a leafy day. Where the hell is he? Is he going to take 37 years to arrive? Did you miss him by four seconds because you had a third slice of toast? Stop flapping. The wonderful thing about the Dream Man is, he wants to find you too.

months. The infuriating thing about the average Dream Man, however, is he often avoids you for years. Worse, when you finally sashay into his line of blue-eyed vision the goon doesn't glance up from his pint. You are reduced to wondering, would you have more success if you exchanged your little black dress for a hops barrel? Enough wondering. Your Dream Man is within reach, and together we'll nail him (in the nicest possible way). We will also have great fun finding him. We are going to travel first class, which means you don't have to trail from bar to bar day in day out, feet raw from tromping, eyes peeled from searching.

Once you've brought Mr Right to heel – and we've got a wealth of strategies to lure him there – the next trick is getting him to sit and stay. Not a problem. Our seductive techniques are easy to master – and so is he. All you require is a little front. Cats do this by fluffing up their tails to make themselves look bigger and more impressive than they really are. Well, as if that fools anyone. We will do it by wile and guile, and the knowledge that if he takes the bait it will be the best thing that ever happened to him. Believe it, go for it, and get him. Then – so long as he does his fair share of the washing up – all will be pink and fluffy for ever. ■

The myth about men fainting at the mere mention of the word commitment is just that – a myth. Men do want to commit – to the right woman – and are only scared of being ridiculed by their jealous single friends, all of whom rely on the pizza delivery boy as their main source of human contact and who haven't had sex with anyone bar their own right hand for eighteen

ANNA PALMA

Thinking
POSITIVE

Positive thinking empowers you, as does a nice pair of boots. We shall employ every ruse possible to ensure that when your eyes finally meet, yours smoulder sexily while his practically pop from their sockets. Begin here...

No, there's nothing half so sweet in life
As love's young dream.

Thomas Moore

SELF-AWARENESS

Do you know what sort of impression you give to other people? It's probably not quite the same as you think.

REAL LIFE, REAL WIRES CROSSED

Tara, 27: 'I'm not very confident but I think of myself as a friendly person. If I feel comfortable I can chat away, but the second I suspect the person I'm talking to isn't captivated, the facade falls away and I stammer and talk nonsense. Recently, I felt as if I was becoming a social pariah. Although I'm successful in my career, when I met up with acquaintances in the same profession I'd feel certain they were regarding me with disdain. I mentioned this to a close friend and she said "Tara, you're a very glamorous woman – but in all honesty you come across as superior and unapproachable. People are in awe of you". I could barely believe it. I think I was so nervous, I wouldn't smile in case someone didn't smile back. Now, I try not to grimace, and to make eye contact. It's made all the difference.'

I WAS SO NERVOUS I WOULDN'T SMILE JUST IN CASE SOMEONE DIDN'T SMILE BACK. NOW I TRY TO MAKE EYE CONTACT AND IT'S MADE ALL THE DIFFERENCE.

Anyone accustomed to speaking in public knows that what you say is only a tiny part of making a good impression. Your audience judges you on your expression, tone, body language, gestures, appearance. In other words, you don't need to burble all night to make him fall for you.

Tape yourself talking and, painful as it is, play it back. If you sound like a sheep calling to its young or a hysterical mouse, train yourself to slow down – this will make your voice less bleaty and/or squeaky. Count the number of times you say 'you know' or 'like' and try to eliminate what you hate about the way you express yourself. If you love every bit of it, hooray for you.

Watch yourself. If you have a habit of say, winking, check in the mirror to ensure you don't make a face like a gargoyle. If your speciality is a Jim Carey style cheesy grin, ditto.

REASSESSING WHAT YOU WANT

Apologies – it sounds like something your mother would say. But it's a great exercise because it makes you consider exactly what you want from a relationship – rather than what you merely think you want – and it works.

Make a list of all your ah, abortive relationships. Beside the name of each man (if you can remember their names!) write down what traits attracted you. In the next column, note down what went wrong. In the next, what was missing from the relationship. In the next, an honest judgement of the reasons. It doesn't matter if you repeat yourself – sometimes asking the same question in slightly different forms is the best way of establishing the truth. See if any patterns emerge from this.

Belinda, 31, who is currently engaged, kissed many a warty toad before finding her dream man. In hindsight, she can see her mistakes – and the motivation for them. Read her story overleaf.

ERIC NCNATT

NAME	ATTRACTION	WHAT WENT WRONG?
Stuart	Good-looking, sheepish, part of a cool crowd, laddish, different background to me.	He seemed to get bored, just stopped calling.
Andrew	Sexy, aloof, very posh (different to me), conservative, amused by me, just split with long-term girlfriend.	We argued – about politics, the role of women, everything. He cheated on me with his ex.
Mike	Cute.	I got bored, he got too serious.
Robert	Irish Catholic, like me.	I didn't fancy him enough, we had our background in common but it was almost too familiar, he was too right-on for me.
Paul	Cool job, amazingly good-looking, laddish, slightly little boy lost.	Emotionally immature, rude to my friends, selfish, I stopped respecting him, I felt like his mother.

WHAT WAS MISSING?	WHY?	BELINDA'S MISTAKE
Depth, real connection.	We didn't have that much in common beyond the initial attraction, too much into his laddish lifestyle to want a serious relationship. I was never part of his crowd.	Maybe I didn't want to see him as he really was. I was shocked when he went off me.
He just saw me as an amusement, not as me, so I adapted my real personality.	Beyond the sex we had zero in common – he was a snob, repressed, he demoralised me.	Thinking I could have a relationship with someone who was aloof – I crave affection, and foolishly, the more he retreated the more I tried to wheedle it out of him. Not having the pride or self-respect to walk away.
Any real interest in him as a person, or respect for him.	He was boring, had nothing to say, he irritated me – his clinginess irritated me.	Choosing looks over personality.
Chemistry.	He was sweet, nice, but it bored me – it was like going out with your brother.	Going out with someone I didn't really fancy.
Any real respect, real compatibility, equality.	He was rubbish at sex, even though I fancied him madly, and his immaturity was frustrating – it made me realise he was too young. I resented him.	Thinking that a guy so into being a lad, who was still rebelling against his parents, would be a suitable partner for me.

Mr Right MARTIN

ATTRACTION   Hysterically funny, intelligent, mischievous, we have great conversations, brilliant in bed, laddish but also mature, very kind and not just to me, cool job, different background but a lot in common – and he is knowledgeable and respectful of my background.

ANY DOUBTS   He was keen on me from the start, which put me off him. Not my usual type – not posh, no emotional problems, no game playing. Good-looking but not lust at first sight for me.

Belinda's conclusion: 'I was a fat, insecure teenager, and for many years I still thought of myself with disgust. I think that was partly the reason why I'd go for men who were wildly different from me, which meant we had nothing in common. I'd also go for emotionally remote men – maybe I thought I didn't deserve love, but it made me miserable when I didn't get it. And the men who were keen on me, like Robert and Mike, I almost despised them for it. I mostly went for looks over personality and I didn't truly respect them as people. It was different with Martin. His personality hooked me. He also makes me feel very loved and great about myself. I am never bored or uncomfortable in his company. I respect him.'

AFTER THE ASSESSMENT

According to the conclusions you reach – and it may be good to ask a trustworthy friend to judge as well – give a man who isn't your normal type a chance, because if you're reading this book it may be that your normal type is the wrong type for you. Some experts suggest this is because you are secretly afraid of commitment so you go for men who you know will eventually reject you, and then you can blame it not working out on them. Consider it. Give the guy you were hum-ha'ing about because he didn't fit your normal criteria a chance. If you want it to be a small chance, make the date a coffee. If the date turns out to be hellish, you can suddenly produce a meeting with your sister in half an hour's time – 'So I'd better leave in ten minutes.' Don't say this as you greet him, because if the date goes stormingly you will have to cut it unnecessarily short.

LEARN TO IGNORE TOXIC ATTITUDES

Such as friends who say things like 'all men are shits'.

CORRECT ANSWER Say nothing but think 'Well, dating a man who refers to women as "rides", drinks 13 pints on a quiet night, and thinks baths are for wusses is bound to colour your judgement. Fortunately, I have better taste than you.'

Don't let miseryguts drag you down. People who say things like this are anathema to securing Mr Right because they clog your head with negative thoughts. If you go out thinking all men are shits (which isn't true, it's an understatement, joke, sorry) you will not give out appropriate vibes. It's easy to be whipped into a self-pitying rant against all men, and certainly, we've all indulged in it and thoroughly enjoyed ourselves. But some women take it too seriously and use it an excuse for eating a whole packet of biscuits in one sitting. Eat the biscuits for heaven's sake – just own up to having a sweet tooth.

The 'all men are shits' attitude is not only juvenile, it is bad for your health. It's the victim mentality – 'Poor me, it's all their fault!' No doubt if miseryguts friend wasn't such a whinging bore she'd get a few more offers. Don't go out with friends like these if you're hoping to stumble across Mr Right because they'll lurk around looking about as jolly as Dracula's shadow and their 'Keep Off' aura will scare away any potential. Not to be mean, but it's not in her interest that you score with a dream man who proves to be sexy, faithful, funny, intelligent, successful, amazing, etc – it would put her theory out of kilter and her nose out of joint.

DEALING WITH ANNOYING ELDERLY RELATIVES

Who say 'What, no young man?' (implication: there's something wrong with you).

CORRECT ANSWER (sweetly smiling) 'No, just one night stands.'

If you stomp away thinking 'Maybe Uncle Dicky is right, maybe I am over the hill, an oddity at 24, because I'm not spending Sundays wheeling a trolley full of cheap tat around a stuffy home store with my devoted man and a diamond on my finger big enough to poke your eye out', you will acquire an air of wild desperation. Remember, when Uncle Dicky was a lad, ladies were considered spinsters if they weren't married by the age of 17. Times have changed since the Victorian era, you might like to inform him. ■

DON'T ALLOW THE NEGATIVE ATTITUDES OF FRIENDS AND THEIR VICTIM MENTALITY TO DRAG YOU DOWN.

Do you have the same kind of negative relationship over and over again? Great news: you can transform your love life.

BREAK YOUR RELATIONSHIP BAD HABITS

(and find true love)

D on't ask me why, but virtually all of my serious relationships have been with Librans – dark-haired, chisel-cheeked Librans at that. In fact, my first serious relationship, some 20 years ago, was with – yes, you've guessed – a raven-haired, chisel-cheeked, kiss-me-I'm-gorgeous Libran. At the same time, all those Librans had an unfortunate tendency to be emotionally cold and somehow unavailable. Just like my father.

All the time I was growing up, my father ignored me. I never once had a family holiday with him, he never took me to the park or played ball, he never tucked me into bed. The effects of having a father who ignored me have been profound. Over and over again, I have been fatally attracted to men who weren't wholly available.

MONICA TREJO

As you can see, relationship history has a habit of repeating itself. We tend to attract, or are attracted to, the same kinds of people. That's what is meant by relationship patterns. There are certain loops women fall into with men. If they're positive, you always choose men who love you, cherish you and treat you like a princess. However, it's the negative patterns that can see us mired in misery.

So how do we fall into these patterns? We first learn about relationships at our mother and father's knees. And from that unfortunate vantage point, our parents seem like gods. They must be right, because we know no different and they seem all-powerful. So we learn from them what love is. We learn from our father what men are like, and we learn from our mother how women should relate to men.

Personally, I have dated many men who were workaholics – just like my father. Certainly, there has always been some challenge, some way of having to work hard to gain their attention – and not always that successfully.

But, if the family relationship has been unhappy, why do we find ourselves attracted to people who resemble our parents or siblings?

*L*OVE NOTE

SEND HIM A HAND-MADE GIFT CERTIFICATE FOR A ONE-HOUR SENSUAL SESSION HE CAN CASH WITH YOU ANY TIME HE WISHES.

The reason we constantly repeat patterns is because we are trying to deal with old traumas. Somewhere, deep down, our subconscious thinks: 'If I can get this bullying, critical man to love me, maybe it will make up for how bullying, critical Daddy never loved me.' Except, of course, bullying, critical men just keep on being what they are – critical bullies – and once again we're broken-hearted.

It's worth asking yourself what your relationship with your parents and siblings was like. Did you have any past experiences that are having a negative influence on your present relationships? You may be able to identify if you are acting out a repetition compulsion of your own.

Of course, all of this is hogwash if you don't do anything about it. But by taking the information from past relationships, and making small steps, you can genuinely change your life. You aren't going to change your personality overnight, but you can begin in small ways. For example, if in past relationships you didn't stand up for yourself, it's likely you don't in other relationships. So, start standing up for yourself with family and close friends. Or if you lost your temper too often, try holding

RK BARRETT

your breath and counting to 10 the next time someone gets your goat.

Every little difference will make you feel inspired and happier with yourself, so you're far less likely to put up with relationships that don't support you, and be attracted to more loving partners in the future. That's why, whether you're in a relationship or single, it's crucial to understand what went wrong with past relationships. Even if you've had happy, successful relationships that just fizzled out, we can always learn more about ourselves and the mistakes we've made.

EVERY LITTLE DIFFERENCE YOU MAKE IN YOUR ATTITUDE TO RELATIONSHIPS WILL MAKE YOU FEEL INSPIRED AND HAPPIER WITH YOURSELF.

It takes just a little private detective work on what went wrong to make sure you don't make the same mistakes again. Taking a cool, honest look at your patterns helps you take responsibility for yourself and your part in the relationship dynamic. It can throw up hidden parts of yourself and it's wonderful for helping you forgive your ex and move on. Oh, and it can save you a bundle in therapist's fees!

Whether you're single, settled or somewhere in between, your new relationship starts here.

WHAT'S YOUR RELATIONSHIP PATTERN?

Use the following questions to assess your relationship history. Your conclusions will reveal the love patterns that are holding you back from finding true happiness.

1 WHO'S YOUR TYPE?

Do you find yourself hooking up with any of these types of men?

● Emotionally unavailable, cold or distant
● Little boys who want you to mother them
● Father figures who are overly protective and stifling
● A challenge – he's either very hard work or just unavailable
● Needs rescuing – he's helpless, shy or bad with money
● Rescuers – great in a crisis, but afterwards always tell you what to do
● Controlling men who won't allow you to live your own life
● Addicted men – to drink, drugs, sex or work
● Abusive men – verbally, physically or sexually
● Unfaithful men
● Commitment-phobes

2 WHAT WAS YOUR EX-PARTNER LIKE?

● What was attractive about him and what couldn't you stand in the end?

3 WHY DID IT END?

● Who ended it and why?
● Have other relationships ended in the same way?

4 WHAT DID YOU DO THAT CONTRIBUTED TO THE BREAK-UP?

Even if your first thought, is 'nothing', use the following questions to see if you notice patterns of behaviour – did you:

● bottle up your anger so it turned to resentment?
● keep losing your temper?
● allow yourself to be bullied?
● believe your partner was always right?
● endure infidelity?
● sleep with someone else?
● avoid intimacy?
● focus on his wants at the expense of your own?
● criticise or nag him?
● always initiate affection?
● indulge in addictions such as excessive drinking?

5 DO YOUR EXES HAVE ANYTHING IN COMMON?

● Think about their positive aspects as well as their negative qualities.

6 WHAT HAVE FAMILY AND FRIENDS SAID ABOUT YOUR PREVIOUS RELATIONSHIPS?

● Ponder the remarks that annoyed you the most – they're often the ones with the kernel of truth you don't want to look at.

7 WAS HE LIKE DADDY?

● Or Mummy? Or a brother or sister, uncle, aunt or favourite teacher? Can you notice patterns in your partner or relationship that reflect patterns in the family you grew up in.

8 WHAT WAS YOUR SEX LIFE LIKE IN YOUR RELATIONSHIPS?

● Did either of you go off sex? Did you have physical difficulties, such as impotence, or was one of you keener than the other?

Your sex life is often a very accurate thermometer for reading the health of a relationship.

KICKSTART YOUR POSITIVE PATTERNS

As we go about our normal, everyday lives, our subconscious file marked 'love' is constantly updated. It gets filled with happy-ever-after fairy stories we read about in books and magazines, the relationships of our parents and friends. It gets added to when our hearts are broken or when we watch a soppy film. And what we learn from all these sources may become our deepest beliefs – beliefs such as 'All men are bastards' or 'I can't be happy on my own'.

LOVE NOTE

BOOK WEEKEND RESERVATIONS AT A HOTEL. WRAP UP THE BROCHURE AND INCLUDE YOUR OWN ITINERARY OF ROMANTIC ACTIVITIES.

ANNE FOUGEDOIRE FERREZ

To change your love patterns you must change these beliefs. Write down a list of your deepest beliefs (including all the small ones) about men and women and relationships. For every negative statement, think of something positive. So:

Negative belief: All men are bastards.

Positive belief: I choose not to believe this. I choose to believe men are basically OK.

Negative belief: I'm hopeless with men.

Positive belief: I choose not to believe this. I choose to believe my relationships are getting better and better all the time.

Repeat these new positive statements on the bus, in the bath, in your lunch break – until they seep into your love file.

Breaking relationship patterns is possible – I know. Until recently, the idea of a loving available man has seemed dull. Then I had a relationship with a man who was more like my father than any man before. But this time there was a difference: I knew I've deserved better and I could let that whole pattern go. The result? At last, I have the relationship I have always dreamed of – with the kind of man I never dreamed I wanted. ■

ALEX CAO

QUIZ

ARE YOU HOLDING OUT FOR A FANTASY MAN?

OR ARE YOU TOO WILLING TO SETTLE?

Would you recognise good marriage material if he were right in front of you on bended knee? Answer these questions to find out if you're setting your sights ridiculously high... or pathetically low.

1 The dinner bill arrives, and your date is short on cash. You:

a Recoil in absolute horror.
b Pay for dinner – and the movie.
c Pick up the tab, but if he doesn't fork out some money next time, he's out.

2 You just found out your new boyfriend has two kids from a previous marriage. You:

a Subtly fish around to see if he's open to the idea of having more.
b Ask whether he's ever considered sending them to boarding school.
c Spend your free time making fudge.

3 Your boss just axed you along with your entire department. Your significant other:

a Doesn't return your tearful calls.
b Immediately picks you up from the office to commiserate over drinks in your favourite bar.
c Drops everything to comfort you. Still, you're annoyed that he doesn't bring a 'recovery holiday' plane ticket.

4 He kisses like a Labrador: lots of slobber, too much tongue. You:

a Give him a smooching lesson.
b Immediately find him a new home.
c Overlook it – he has so many other good qualities to concentrate on.

5 His hair has been thinning the past few months. You:

a Bail out. In your book, bald ain't beautiful.
b Stick by him. Bruce Willis is way sexier than Ginola any day.
c Ignore it – and his growing spare tyre.

6 Your new man goes mad every time you get together with your male friends. You:

a Think it's sweet. He must really care.
b Get an ex-directory number right away. What'll be next – stalking?
c Sit him down and reassure him that these guys are just friends.

7 He's been spending a lot of time at his high-stress new job. The best way to deal?

a Tell him to take an immediate holiday – or you're history.
b Let it slide – he hates it when you nag.
c Compromise. You will be more understanding about his long hours if he'll be more responsive at home.

8 Now you've been living together for a while, you're not having sex so often – though you feel closer to him than ever. You:

a Don't panic. Every relationship has dry spells.
b Look elsewhere.
c Hardly notice. You weren't that physically attracted to him in the first place.

9 He tells you he cannot imagine ever settling down with just one woman. You:

a Wait a while to see if he changes his mind. If he doesn't come around soon,

you'll make tracks.
b Tell him that you're crazy about him, and if you have to share him, so be it.
c Figure he's not worth your time. If he were, he'd sacrifice his little black book for you, pronto.

10 On those crucial first few dates, he should be willing to:

a Talk about anything, including his most embarrassing moments. How else can you get to know him?
b Discuss what moves him. And if it's the Premiership race, well, you're just happy to have a man who'll talk.
c Tell you a bit about his family, his future plans and hopes. Anything more would be too much too soon.

LOVE NOTE

MAKE HIM FEEL SPECIAL. SEND HIM FLOWERS, CHAMPAGNE OR WHISKEY, WITH A SEXY NOTE EXPLAINING WHAT YOU'D LIKE TO DO TO HIM.

11 You were stuck late at work every night last week. Your mate:

a Had you up until midnight cooking dinner – he likes things just so.

b Took over all the household duties without your even asking.

c Was thoughtless – he didn't iron and made the most uninspiring meals.

12 Tick any of these you agree with:

a You'd never date a guy who's not taller than you.

b You can tinker with a man, but you can't overhaul him completely.

c Every time one of your friends announces her engagement, you panic.

d You don't expect your future husband to support you financially.

e If sparks don't fly on the first date, you don't accept (or ask for) a second.

f You've had lots of brief romances.

g You like a guy who's unpredictable.

h You drop your friends when you become seriously involved with a man.

ANNE FOUGEDOIRE FERREZ

SCORING

1	a–3	b–1	c–2
2	a–2	b–3	c–1
3	a–1	b–2	c–3
4	a–2	b–3	c–1
5	a–3	b–2	c–1
6	a–1	b–3	c–2
7	a–3	b–1	c–2
8	a–2	b–3	c–1
9	a–2	b–1	c–3
10	a–3	b–1	c–2
11	a–1	b–2	c–3

12 Give yourself the corresponding number for each item ticked.

a–1	b–2	c–1	d–2
e–3	f–3	g–1	h–1

Now count up the number of 1s, 2s and 3s you've ticked – but don't add them together.

MOSTLY 1s:
Beavis and Butt-head Groupie

So what if he insists on splitting the bill with you at McDonald's? Since you can't imagine doing any better, you don't bother looking for someone who understands the finer points of romance and intimacy. Unconsciously, you may be trying to re-create an unhappy or deprived child-hood, says psychologist Alan Entin. 'People who treat you poorly feel comfortable and familiar,' he explains. You may also desperately fear getting hurt, adds psychologist Carl Hindy. 'You figure you can't be rejected by someone so pathetic.'

So, how to stop reeling in bottom-feeders? Ask your friends and family to help by telling you what they really think of the unemployed tattoo artist you've been seeing. 'Grill them early on in the relationship – when they feel they can be honest,' advises Hindy. Should that fail, consider therapy as a means of figuring out what fuels your loser lust.

MOSTLY 2s:
The Good-Guy Girl

You don't demand perfection. If he forgets to put the toilet seat back down, that's okay, as long as he meets more fundamental needs. On the other hand, a man who constantly nags you to lose five pounds won't last long with you – which doesn't mean you'll never compromise for him; if he can't stand your wet undies hanging all over the flat, you'll clean up your act. As for sex, you're realistic enough not to ditch him once the initial thrill is gone. 'You understand chemistry counts,' says Entin, 'but also that the key to a long-lasting relationship is friendship.'

MOSTLY 3s:
Mrs Pitt Wanna-be

Sorry, Brad Pitt is taken. But given the chance, you'd probably find plenty wrong with him. A fear of intimacy may be why you always set your sights too high. 'You look for a fatal flaw to avoid engaging in a real relationship,' says Entin. Or perhaps your self-esteem's so low, you subconsciously think, 'If I'm with him, people will think I'm worth something.' In either case, says Entin, a little self-exploration (alone or with a therapist) may help free you from your quest for the ideal man. In the meantime, if your head says he's a good guy, give your heart a chance to catch up. ∎

Be an Ace
AT SMALL TALK

Getting just the right balance between
asking questions, being a good listener
and talking yourself can be tricky,
especially if you're nervous. You don't
want to overwhelm him with questions,
but then again, you don't want to keep
talking about me, me, me. We've put
together a few suggestions for you.

NICKY JOHNSTON

- Don't finish his sentences for him.
- Don't nod like a nodding dog as if you're desperate for him to hurry up and stop talking.
- Although men like to talk about themselves there is a difference between asking questions and interrogation.
- Don't be too nosy – even if you disguise it with nice words it's still plain nosiness, for example, 'I hope you don't mind me asking, but how much would you pay for a flat like that?'

- If you want to draw him out, ask open-ended questions – for instance, if he says he's just been to the US on holiday, a smart woman would say 'How exciting, which bit? Did you have a nice time?' Then follow up with 'What did you do?' Thus giving her talking partner permission to expand. A bad conversationalist would shut him up before he's even started by saying, 'I go to the US quite often on business' – which effectively puts a great big verbal bar in the

ANNA PALMA

way of him opening up about him because you force him (if he has any social nouse whatsoever) to ask about you: 'Oh, right. What do you do?'

● Also, if possible, try to avoid closed questions that elicit a one-word answer. Ask open questions that provoke an emotional response. For example, rather than say 'Do you like *The Sweeney*?' (he says 'Yes'), ask 'Why do you like *The Sweeney*?' (he says 'Where shall I begin?').

● Don't put wit above the conversational flow. For example, he says 'I'm feeling very smug – I'm the best man at a wedding this weekend – nothing to wear, walked into Oswald Boeteng, amazing suit, reduced to half price, flash of the card and I'm all set!' You could respond 'Sounds gorgeous – whose wedding?' Or you could say 'Ah, but does it fit you?!'

● Talk about yourself but if he asks you a question you don't want to answer, don't. Just laugh and say nothing. Or, say 'None of your business sweetie.'

● Don't ramble on to fill a silence. Some men keep quiet on purpose to gain the upper hand. Don't fall for such a low-down trick. You're likely to say something silly and it makes you look nervous. If you've said what you want to say, shut up and wait for him to speak.

TRY NOT TO ASK QUESTIONS THAT PROVOKE A SIMPLE 'YES' OR 'NO' ANSWER. ASK OPEN QUESTIONS TO ENCOURAGE CONVERSATION.

BE TOUGH AGAINST REJECTION

What's the worst thing that can happen? You think he's up for it – you've been flirting shamelessly all night, he's been giving you all the signs – yet when you say 'So, do you want to meet up sometime?' he steps back, looks aghast, claps his hands loudly and shouts 'Everyone! Guess what! This woman (points finger, everyone stares) thinks I want to go out with her and I don't!' Then, everyone in the room laughs uproariously at you because you fancied him and he didn't fancy you back so obviously you had ideas above your station, and what makes you think you're so special etc, etc.

When rejected, this is how it can feel. Instead of thinking 'More fool you,' we wonder what's wrong with us. But 'More fool you' should be the stock response inside your head. We won't pretend that rejection is anything other than one of the most misery-making things in the world. But if you want to nab Mr Right, dealing with rebuffs from Mr Wrong in a positive way is vital.

First, establish why he may have rejected you:

● He doesn't know you but he thinks you're not right for him.

● He's going out with someone.

● He does know you, but he thinks you're not right for him.

● He doesn't fancy you.

PEPTALK

When faced with rejection, just remember these points:

- He doesn't know you – so he's not rejecting you as a person; he simply doesn't know the true wonder of you.
- It's not personal – he's already spoken for. Pity the woman he's going out with that he has to flirt excessively with others to satisfy his ego.
- If he does know you: he thinks the two of you would not be suited as a couple. This doesn't mean he thinks you're worthless/boring etc, it means he doesn't think you're right for him. He's entitled to his opinion, and maybe he's right. None of us are right for lots of people – even, regretfully, Matt Dillon or Matt Le Blanc. Even if you envy the great relationship your good friend has with her fiancé, you wouldn't want to marry him.
- While many men in this world fancy Kate Moss, some men think 'Ugh – too skinny, pointy nose,' and prefer the curves of Sophie Dahl, which is to say, whatever you look like, not every man in the world is going to fancy you. It's nothing personal, it's just reality. Instead, concentrate on thinking of the men who did/do fancy you.

$\mathscr{L}$OVE NOTE

PERFECT YOUR MANNERS. IT'S A WELL-KNOWN FACT THAT BEAUTIFUL MANNERS CAN BE SUPER-SEXY.

EXTRA NOTE

Why should this man's decision have any bearing on your self-estimation? If you feel American-minded enough, write a list of, say, five wonderful things people have said to you that made you feel great. What he thinks doesn't change you in any way. You are exactly the same person you were this morning – you are not, suddenly, a worse person.

If he rejects you in a demeaning way, he's confirmed he's a moron. Excellent – once you have smoothed your ruffled feathers, this will hasten your recovery as you will be forced to admit to yourself that he's a berk. Because, unless you have been stalking him (stalking lite doesn't count – see page 58) or behaving badly yourself – there is no excuse for nastiness. It doesn't reflect on you, it reflects on him. We are only spiteful to people if something they are/have/do makes us uncomfortably aware of something we lack.

PLAIN EXAMPLE

When Susanna, 25, announced her engagement, her colleagues were thrilled for her. Except one person, Martine. Martine's response was 'You're mad. You're making a mistake. You're far too young to

ANNE FOUGEDOIRE FERREZ

ERIC MCNATT

get married.' My, my, a confident
person might have thought – why
so touchy? Susanna, however,
didn't think 'What's wrong with her
that she isn't pleased for me, like a
normal friend?' She thought, 'Maybe
I am too young.' She confided in
her good friend Laura who asked
for a little information about
Martine. Susanna: 'Well, she's
separated from her husband, who
left her for another woman.' Hmm.
Why is there no mystery here?

THE POINT

If a man rejects you in a cruel way
(for example he reacts snidely if
you ask him to dance, your most
dignified reply is a cool 'There's no
need to be rude.'), his behaviour
suggests he has a problem, as do
the following scenarios:

● He just doesn't call = weak,
cowardly, juvenile.
● You ask him to dance, he says
'not with you' = insecure about

You sleep with him once, he slags you off = his pathetic bedroom performance has never been challenged, whereas you as a woman who knows what she wants, recognises quality and doesn't put up with less makes him aware of his inadequacies; he has a mental age of ten; strong women scare him because ultimately he's weak and insecure.

OVERALL VERDICT
Thank him for saving you from wasting your time.

PEPTALK
Every time some dufus turns you down, you're one man nearer to the perfect one who says 'I like everything about you, please may I keep you?'

There are a squillion toads out there and probably only one-tenth of a squillion princes. The joyous thing is, you only need one prince. Even better, some toads, when they meet the right woman, miraculously turn into princes.

There's no such thing as 'All the good men are spoken for' – some wonderful men, like some equally wonderful women, meet their perfect partner aged 32 or 42, not 22.

So just hang in there – and try to enjoy yourself while you're looking for that prince. ■

FOR EVERY MAN WHO SAYS NO, YOU'RE ONE MAN CLOSER TO FINDING THE PERFECT ONE.

masculinity; immature; has to make himself look hard and big by making others look small; has a miniscule penis (medical terminology: matchstick dick).

You make conversation, he replies in monosyllables = socially inept; possibly badly brought up; shallow; vain.

He leads you on, until weeks later you realise he's not interested = control freak; emotional hang-ups; cold nature.

WHAT *not* TO SAY ON A FIRST MEETING

So you've finally managed to get him alone for a moment. You have one chance to make that all-important first impression and you're nervous. Well, that's completely understandable, but please, do try not to say the first thing that comes into your mind, such as…

● 'I'll stick to orange juice, I've got a terrible period pain, really heavy flow, it feels like it's dragging my whole uterus out of my body, I get really bloated, it's agony, alcohol makes it worse.'

● 'Yeah, that's my plan – marry someone rich then retire, ha ha!'

● 'Well, Bunnee-Pinkums sleeps on the pillow, and Wuffer-Puffer sleeps next to her – then BaaLamb gets at least a foot of the bed to herself, also she doesn't get on well with Mr Whisker so they have to be separated…'

IT'S IMPORTANT TO STAND UP TO HIS FRIENDS, BECAUSE IF THEY DISLIKE YOU, THEY'LL LET HIM KNOW. THIS MEANS REFUSING TO LET THEM UPSET YOU, EVEN IF THEY ARE A BUNCH OF NEANDERTHALS.

'My ex, what a psycho, he once locked me in a cupboard for three hours because he said I was freaking him out by nagging him too much, god I hate men like that, what a loony, sometimes, if he ran out of clean underwear, he'd wear the same pair of pants two days in a row, he'd turn then inside out, disgusting, I mean, can you believe that? And sometimes when he breathed his nose squeaked.'

'Well, as my mother says…'

'Oh 30 at least! I was a late starter but once I got going, well, ha ha, there was no stopping me, let's see, Mark, blond well-built if you get my drift, but it didn't last – the relationship I mean, he personally could go on and on, then there was Luke, tall, slightly overweight but something to hold on to, know what I mean!'

'You don't look very strong.'

'So you went out with her for precisely how long? And what's her name? And exactly what does she look like? And what does she do? And was she good in bed? And how often do you see her? And where does she live? And is she going out with anyone? And do you still fancy her? And is she prettier than me?'

MAKE STRONG EYE CONTACT – HOLDING HIS GAZE FOR SEVERAL UNINTERRUPTED SECONDS CAN BE VERY EROTIC AND INTIMATE.

'I didn't get on with my father, you see, so after the anorexia, I was in and out of clinics, I suppose I was improving but when my aunt died I just lost it, I started cutting myself – nothing serious, just a few scratches but it's a downhill slope, so I was seeing a psychiatrist, but I didn't think much of him, so I was referred to someone else, he was much better, but then…'

'Accountancy – poor you!'

'How much do you earn?'

'Oh I dunno. I just feel [sigh] as if I'm a bit of a failure. I mean [sigh] I hate my job, and I'd really like to do something more interesting and like, maybe, travel a bit, but [sigh] that means I'd need to find lodgers for my flat and [sigh] I don't know if I'd get my old job back when I came back – I mean, I know I said I hate it, and I do, but [sigh] well, it's just so hard, y'know.'

AND THIS IS WHAT YOU CAN SAY…
What he says: 'You look the sporty type.'
What he means: You have a great body – I bet you can go on and on.

What you say: 'Well, I surf and kickbox. It's more fun than exercise.'

What you don't say: 'It's all down to hard work – I don't eat junk food, and I'm teetotal, and I won't drink caffeine, honestly it's so bad for you, it's been linked with cancer, and I do the Mr Motivator workout every morning and twice a day at weekends.'

What he says: 'You have a filthy laugh.'
What he means: I bet you're a right tiger when you get going.

What you say: 'That's not the half of it darling.' [laugh]
What you don't say: 'Oh no, it just sounds like that today because of my laryngitis.'

What he says: 'You have very expressive hands.'
What he means: You seem like an enthusiastic, lively, sensual person.

What you say: 'That's what my ex-boyfriend used to say.'
What you don't say: 'That's what my flute tutor says.'

What he says: 'You look Italian, or Spanish.'

What he means: You look, exotic, exciting, interesting.

What you say: 'Well, I speak Italian'* or 'My family is originally from Sicily.'**
What you don't say: 'Nah, sorry, Wolverhampton born and bred.'

* Don't say this if the only words you know in Italian are *penne arrabiata*. If you do speak Italian, it's worth about 50 points – in manspeak: 'A bird who speaks Italian, fwaor!'
** Again, would be nice if it were true, but if it's not and he asks too many questions, explain that your great-great-grandfather, whose surname was, ah, Barberi, emigrated to Wolverhampton and the name Barberi then got anglicised to, er, Horncastle. Worth about 30 points – in manspeak: 'A bird with mafia connections…' ∎

*L*OVE NOTE

WRITE 'I LOVE YOU' IN GRAPES, CHOCOLATE BUTTONS OR WHATEVER HE LOVES BEST ON THE KITCHEN TABLE.

The sleepless nights
The daily fights
The quick toboggan
when you hit the heights
I miss the kisses
and I miss the bites
I wish I were in love again.

Rodgers/Hart,
as sung by Ella Fitzgerald

WAYS TO DISTINGUISH
the Wheat from the Chaff

Or sussing out who's an idiot and who's a nice guy disguised as an idiot.

OPENING REMARKS
- Boo: he's said, 'What do you do?' You tell him and he says, 'Really, well that's funny because I... and I... when I... etc, etc.'
- Hooray: he's said, 'What do you do?' You tell him and he says, 'Really, that sounds interesting, how did you...?' etc, etc.
- Why?: if he's really interested in you he won't immediately turn everything you say into an excuse to bark on about himself.

APPEARANCE
- Boo: he's wearing a home-knitted jumper which – amid the garish pattern – is splattered in egg-stains.
- Hooray: he's wearing a scruffy unironed shirt and his trousers have seen better days.

- Why?: anyone over the age of 14 is too old to wear jumpers knitted by granny in a public place. Strongly suggests he is immature and, judging by the egg stains, can't be bothered to look after himself and needs mothering. Scruffiness, however, is excusable – that's just bloke nature. As long as his clothes are clean.

SMELL
- Boo: slight whiff of BO.
- Hooray: little heavy on the aftershave.
- Why?: with modern plumbing and a vast range of sanitary products on the market he has no excuse to smell bad. Shows a selfish disregard for other people and a shocking lack of self-awareness. Too much after-shave doesn't have to mean he's a smooth cad, who of course would be wearing just the right amount. Possibly a little insecure and out on the pull. That's all you need to know, surely?

HAIR
- Boo: flamboyant sideburns and slightly bouffed.
- Hooray: shockingly short.
- Why?: any man with showoffy sideburns is dealing with some issue you don't want to be any part of – either he is bitter at taking his parents' advice and becoming a lawyer rather than a rock star or he is insecure with his masculinity and obsessed with the concept of balding and thinks no one will notice his bare pate if he covers his face with bumfluff. Bouffing is equally bad news (Michael Flatley – need we say more?) Short, however, is on the whole good, even if it isn't flattering. Either he has a refreshing lack of vanity (doesn't know a salon tragedy when he sees one) or has confronted his receding hairline in a healthy, stylish way. Consider the alternative: a comb-over. ■

NOEL J FEDERIZO

What if it's You
WHO WANTS HIM?

'I NEVER ASKED A MAN OUT UNTIL I WAS 30. THEREFORE I ONLY WENT OUT WITH MEN WHO ASKED ME, AND A FRIEND POINTED OUT THAT I WASN'T DOING THE PICKING. ALSO I THOUGHT, IT'S ALWAYS BEEN TRADITIONAL THAT MEN ASK US OUT, BUT NOTHING'S TRADITIONAL ANY MORE SO WHY NOT GIVE IT A GO? SO I ASKED A GUY OUT I HAD MY EYE ON AND WE ENDED UP GOING OUT FOR SIX MONTHS. THESE DAYS I HAVE NO SHAME – I ASK MEN OUT ALL THE TIME – AND THEY LOVE IT...'

Rosa, on taking destiny into her own hands

It's a minefield, showing someone you find them attractive. A survey by Dateline found only 23 per cent of men and 37 per cent of women find it easy to approach strangers. And approaching someone you already know can be even trickier.

Surfing the Internet on dating, I came across a book called *Baby, All Those Curves and Me With No Brakes: 500 New No-Fail Pick-Up Lines for Men And Women*. I don't know about you, but my likely reply to that opening gambit would be: Baby, All That Chat and Me With No Ears. Here are a few ways of getting your message across without getting into trouble. Or, maybe getting into the best kind of trouble.

WAYS OF APPROACHING A MAN

The best advice is to keep it simple. If you work with him, keep asking him questions related to work until one day you ask if he'd like to discuss it all over a quick drink in the bar round the corner from the office. (Or, if you can, email asking him out for a drink. The written word spares your blushes.) If you spy him at the gym, ask how to use a particular piece of equipment. Or ask a man in the video shop to recommend a funny film.

Take the story of Katherine, who mooned over a man at work from afar for months, until she decided it was high time she changed her tactics:

■ Every Monday I'd make a point of asking him what he had done at the weekend. It never seemed to involve anything of the girlfriend variety, so one time, when he said he'd been to the cinema I said, bold as you like, 'Why don't we go to see a film?' He instantly went bright red and said 'I'd love that, I'll look in the paper and see what's on and we'll make a date'. It turned out that he'd liked me for ages but was actually quite insecure and didn't think I'd ever be interested in him.

OPEN UP YOUR MIND COMPLETELY TO NEW IDEAS AND WAYS OF APPROACHING MEN. REPLACE ANY NEGATIVE THOUGHTS WITH 'I'M GOING TO ENJOY THIS'.

IF YOU DON'T KNOW HIM...

Cosmo tried some pick-up lines which they practised on men on the street, in bars and so on. They went like this:

● 'Hey, Mark! Oh, I'm sorry – I thought you were someone else.'
● 'My brother's birthday is next week and he wants some new trainers. Can I ask you where you got yours?'
● 'I see you here a lot. Would you mind if I bought you a drink?'
● 'I know this seems forward, but my friend just bet me £5 I wouldn't have the nerve to introduce myself to you. My name is...'
● 'Do you know a good coffee shop round here? I'm gasping.'

These all, apparently, led to conversations and even an exchange of phone numbers.

FINDING OUT IF HE'S AVAILABLE

Other women's men are off-limits, even if it's them doing the chasing. Here are the tips for digging out availability clues – and how to have fun with them:

● A wedding ring – look at third finger, left hand.
● A ring on any other finger: you

could ask if it's a wedding ring and see what kind of reply you get. Then you can subtly follow it up with 'Are you attached?'

● Ask him where he lives, then 'Do you live with anyone?'

● Ask him what he did at the weekend. If he offers no leading clues, come straight out with it and say: 'Did you go with your girlfriend?'

● If all these are just too subtle and you still haven't found out the crucial information, stare at the space just above the guy's right ear and boldly say: 'So, are you seeing anyone?'

If all this quizzing doesn't give him the hint and get him asking you out, and you're still determined to hook this particular fish, you'll just have to do it yourself.

REMEMBER IT'S THE TWENTY-FIRST CENTURY AND YOU'RE AN INDEPENDENT WOMAN – IF YOU WANT SOMETHING, GO AFTER IT.

HOW TO ASK A MAN OUT SO HE'LL SAY YES!

OK, maybe you've done all of the above and he's obviously terminally shy or hideously slow. Or maybe you glimpsed him once across a crowded room and won't see him again unless you engineer it. Or maybe last time you saw him you were with someone and now you're not and he won't know that.

So ask him out, already. It's the twenty-first century. All those rules about the man has to do the asking are so last century. If you want something, go get it girl. He may be the love of your life.

ON THE PHONE:

Advantage: He can't see you blushing. Or your best friend giggling in the corner. You've also

got an easy backout if he says no.
Disadvantage: You have to know his phone number. You might catch him at a bad moment.

VIA EMAIL
Advantage: He can't see you blushing, he can't hear the nervousness in your voice. If he says no, the two of you need never even mention it.
Disadvantage: Technological gremlins which sweep your message into a communication black hole; if he doesn't reply you still don't know where you stand.

IN THE FLESH
Advantage: You get to smile, flirt, pout and indulge every alluring body language thing you know.
Disadvantage: It's harder if he says no.

ASK HIM ALONG TO A GROUP THING
Like a party, a softball game.
Advantage: It's casual. There are other people there.
Disadvantage: He may not realise it's a date. He may not turn up. He may get off with your best friend.

THE BET TECHNIQUE
This one can't lose apparently, but it only works if you meet at a party, or at work or some other social situation and is obviously no use for Mr Across-a-Crowded-Room.

It works like this: pounce on a piece of trivia you and Mr Cute have bonded over in your conversation. Song lyrics, Italian football players, whatever – as long as it's provable. Then bring up a point of dispute and say: 'Loser takes winner out to dinner'. If he agrees, you're checking into Date Central. If he says, no way, you know he's not interested.

It's a win/win situation. No matter who loses, you still get to go out to dinner.

RK BARRETT

WHAT IF HE'S A FRIEND?

This is an extremely common, extremely tricky dating dilemma. You've spent time cultivating your male friendship – after all, every girl needs a platonic male friend – then you find yourself feeling more than ordinarily friendly. The question is, does he?

You're only going to find out if you say something. And if you say something, there are real risks. You may lose a valuable friendship, which has a high level of emotional investment. You risk rejection (after all, he hasn't said anything to indicate how he feels). And you risk the embarrassment factor of all your other friends finding out afterwards.

First, you need to weigh up whether it's worth it, remembering that, after all, true friendship is the basis of any love relationship worth having.

Ask yourself how serious you are about promoting him from friend to boyfriend, think about what signs you've had from him. And if you decide all in all, it is worth it, set about using every weapon in your flirting arsenal. Apply everything you know about body language. Compliment him. Hint rather than coming straight out with it.

Mary had been friends with a work colleague, David, for a year when the office Christmas party rolled round. They were chatting as usual, then had a dance. A slow record came on, they moved towards one another – and that was that. She says: 'It was electric. He said, "Shall we leave?" And we did and we've been together ever since. But neither of us were conscious of liking each other in that way until they played that Marvin Gaye song.'

But what if non-verbal communication doesn't work? You might choose to bite the bullet and say: 'Do you know I find you attractive?' If he says something like, 'Yes, but you're Elaine', then you know where you stand.

If he says, 'Sorry, but I don't see you in that way', you can say something light-hearted like, 'Never mind, we can still be friends' and have a little private late-night sob into your pillow later. It is very grown-up to acknowledge a mutual attraction, even if you don't (or can't) do anything about it.

And if he runs away and just can't cope with it, what kind of a friend was he anyway? Then again, you might end up happy ever after. Good luck! ■

*L*OVE NOTE

DURING A CANDLE-LIT DINNER *A DEUX*, PLAY SMOOCHY TUNES, SUCH AS FRANK SINATRA'S *SONGS FOR SWINGING LOVERS.*

TAMARA SCHLESINGER

VAN QUANG

HOW TO
Seduce Him

MAKING
Contact

The pomp and puffery that surround the idea of men and women who don't know each other meeting in a public place for the first time, acknowledging each other and (gasp!) striking up a conversation, is bizarre. On the pull... cattle market... getting picked up... Yes, and? It's natural! We'd be extinct otherwise! What possible gripe can anyone have about someone wanting to find The One? Thanks to all the hype, searching for Mr Right can chill you with fear. In fact, it's a blast, so prepare to dazzle.

ERIC MCNATT

THE DIRECT APPROACH FOR NO-NONSENSE WOMEN

Wait until he trots off to the bar (i.e. away from his friends, as men live to make it difficult for their friends to score) then sidle up, on the pretext of buying a drink, and ask him any question you can think of. The object of this is not to be devastatingly witty – save that till later – it is to bring to his attention the fact that you exist.

So, ask him anything – from the very plain, obvious but functional 'Do you have the time/a light?/both?' to the more daring but rather cute 'Is it hot in here or is it just you?'

Some (American) experts advise sauntering up and saying 'I love your shirt, may I ask where you got it – I need to get a birthday present for my brother.' Fine, but only if you can say it slinkily and without looking as if you know he knows you both know it's a great fat lie you've concocted in order to talk to him.

In the interests of research, a friend tested this line. The man in question looked at her in a raised eyebrow kind of way and she giggled. He then said 'That's just a line, isn't it?' She confessed and said 'Well, if you must know, my brother is ten!' – and he grinned and bought her a drink and – to date – they are very happy together. It's whatever you think will work with him.

THE EVEN MORE DIRECT APPROACH

Perhaps you don't have the time or patience to play games. Still, wait till he is at a safe distance from his friends. Then – perhaps at the bar – say, 'I know you're with friends but I'd really like to buy you a drink. May I?' This approach – excessively polite, but not grovelling or apologetic – prompts a number of responses: the teasing 'Of course you may,' or (after an appraising glance) 'No, let me buy *you* a drink.' The drink line is less portentous than 'Would you like to go out with me?' (hello? a second ago I didn't even know you existed) but effectively it means the same thing.

HOORAY NOTE

I have it on good male authority that if a woman approached a man in this way, the only way he'd turn her down was if he was with his girlfriend – yawn, au revoir – or he was drinking with a friend he hadn't seen in ten years and whose death was imminent. And then – this is a

*L*OVE NOTE

VISIT THE NEAREST FAIRGROUND AND KISS FOR THE ENTIRE DURATION OF THE ROLLERCOASTER.

direct quote – 'You'd regretfully say "Can you come back tomorrow, my friend's about to die – he'll be dead by five, can we have a drink at 6.30 – there's a pub I know near the hospital…" '

If, however, and more likely, he is drinking with friends he sees week in, week out and who, despite their habits, seem destined for a reasonably long life – 'You'd ditch them in a shot and walk off with your thumb in the air because you've pulled.' Ah, so it's not exactly dignified for the woman then? Would he lose respect for her? 'No, you'd be thinking "Thank you for saving me the trouble of asking you. If only all women were like that." '

BOTHER NOTE

Beware – this Judas to the male sex adds a cautionary note: 'It does make you big-headed and think "She fancies me so I don't have to do so much."'

OUR VERDICT

You only have to stand behind some men in a queue and they think you're after them (well, you are, in a sense). So, what do you care? You've practically got a date! Also, even if he asked you first, the fact that you said 'Yes, I'd like a gin and tonic please,' will also make him think, 'She fancies me... I've

YOUR AIM IS FOR THE MAN YOU ARE INTENT ON TO BE SITTING WITH YOU, GAZING INTO YOUR EYES AND GRINNING LIKE THE CHESHIRE CAT ON PROZAC.

pulled.' At this stage, don't concern yourself about how far he thinks he's going to get with you, possibly tonight, just because you made the first move. The point is – the man you are intent on is sitting with you, gazing into your eyes and grinning like the Cheshire cat on Prozac. Admittedly, he is the one in control as he is more certain of your feelings than you of his. Let him enjoy his shortlived triumph. He is putty.

CHILDISH BUT EFFECTIVE WAYS TO EVEN THINGS OUT

● Just as he's thinking 'I wish I'd changed the sheets in the last quarter,' you bring the drink to an end by kissing him demurely on the cheek, shoving your business card into his pocket, saying 'Thanks for the drink – give me a call,' and sashaying elegantly out of the door (just make sure you don't ruin the effect by tripping over the step).

● Say 'Thanks for that – I really enjoyed it. But I'd better get back to my friends.' Then kiss him on the cheek – near the mouth, but on the cheek – and walk away. There is a 95% chance he will sheepishly wander over later – or if he's playing it safe, corner you when you are next at the bar – and ask for your number.

PERSONAL SPACE ALERT

However you wangled it, you and he are yakking. But don't stand too close to him. People get touchy about invasion of their personal space – it's partly why everyone is so growly on the Tube. Invading someone's space is an aggressive, insensitive thing to do and it makes people hostile. Furthermore, men like to think of themselves as predators. So, if you are talking to him and you decide to stand three inches from his face before he has inched towards you, he may subconsciously think you are chasing him (absurd thought) and he may consciously feel a rise of irritation towards you. Let him be the one to step towards you. You simply don't need to move a muscle, sweetie.

WHEN YOU KNOW WHO YOU WANT: STALKING LITE

Engineer the meeting by research. Find out where he likes to hang out, and start hanging out there. Bribe a girlfriend, or a few, to accompany you. Your goal should be to have fun irrespective of whether he turns up. Although he is the reason you are staking out the Pig & Pen, don't spend the entire night glancing over your shoulder towards the door.

Get there relatively early so you can park yourselves at a

WHEN OUT ON THE HUNT, DO TRY NOT TO LOOK LIKE A MYOPIC VULTURE, PEERING RAVENOUSLY AROUND THE ROOM, LOOKING SOMEWHAT DESPERATE AND SAD.

conspicuous table, get the drinks in, and enjoy yourselves. This strategy gives you a double advantage: he will very possibly spot you first – indeed, nearly all men frequenting the pub will spy you from your superb attention-grabbing spot. When he does spy you, you will not resemble a myopic vulture, peering ravenously round the room (which always looks desperate and slightly sad). You will be laughing becomingly and (heheh) unselfconsciously with your gal pals over some impossibly witty remark...

Back down to earth – that said men are almost unbelievably bad at spotting you when you want them to. Thus, each girlfriend, yourself included of course, will periodically leave the table to go to the toilet or order more drinks – in reality to scour the crowds in search of your prey, and report back. ∎

TAMARA SCHLESINGER

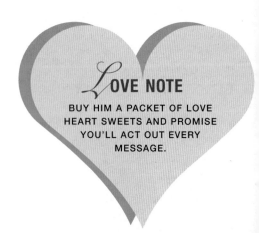

LOVE NOTE

BUY HIM A PACKET OF LOVE HEART SWEETS AND PROMISE YOU'LL ACT OUT EVERY MESSAGE.

Pursue-you RULES

It's time to let him do all the chasing. So here are the eight tricks you need to make sure he crosses the room to charm you.

● ●

You're standing in a crowded bar and you spot the man of your dreams across the room. Or, perhaps you already know someone who makes you go weak at the knees and he's going to be at the same party as you tonight. So what do you do? Of course you have the confidence to make the first move – but wouldn't it be great if you didn't have to? If you possessed such irresistible appeal that men were simply drawn to you? Well, it is possible.

'If you're aware of ways to make yourself more alluring, you'll be able to attract men and make them approach you,' says psychologist Dr Peter Bull, an expert in interpersonal communication at the University of York. 'Knowing how to give off certain signals gives you the self-possession and confidence that men find difficult to resist.'

To point you in the right direction, Cosmo has enlisted the best experts on the male mind to reveal the rules that will make him pursue you...

PURSUE-YOU RULE 1

Dress like a diva

If you want him to sit up and take notice, the shade that will really grab his attention is purple. 'It gets you noticed because it's a strong colour that makes the wearer look confident and classy,' says says image adviser Cliff Bashforth of colour consultancy Colour Me

Beautiful. 'Magenta also has a lot of pulling power because it makes you stand out from the crowd. It has energy which is why it affects the way people respond to you. Earthy colours such as greens or browns are a definite turn-off because they drain and intimidate,' he adds.

Once the colour's caught his eye, reel him in with the next trick – strokeability! Wear clothes in tactile fabrics and his subconscious will be telling him to move closer and touch you. Cashmere, velvet and butter-soft suede all score highly on the stroke-me scale. And the trick is to emphasise your assets. Identify the most beautiful part of your body and show it off. For

TAMARA SCHLESINGER

example if you love your ankles, go for the strappiest shoes with high heels.

PURSUE-YOU RULE 2

Tempt with your tresses

Forget spending hours in front of the mirror with a truckload of styling products – according to the experts, men go weak at the knees for the slightly messy look. 'Men love long, tumbling tresses with a slightly bedraggled look – Jennifer Lopez's hair is the perfect example,' says celebrity hairstylist Michael Cimino of Schreiber Woodall Hair, whose clients include actress Sadie Frost. 'Having a long fringe that just covers one eye is also one of the sexiest looks a woman can have because it's so mysterious and seductive,' he continues. 'Whatever the style, so long as you have attitude and carry it off with confidence, men will notice you,' concludes Cimino.

But getting the guys to chase you isn't just about how you wear your hair: what you do with it is equally important. 'Playing with your hair is a preening signal to men that says "notice me",' says Peta Heskell, author of *Flirt Coach* (HarperCollins). 'Twirl your hair around your fingers while arching your back and you'll really catch his eye.'

I shudder at the sight of men I'm due to fall in love again.

Dorothy Parker

RK BARRETT

PURSUE-YOU RULE 3

Exude confidence

Looking self-assured – even if you're quaking in your spike heels – is a sure-fire way to have guys making a beeline for you. You need to exude total come-to-me confidence from the moment you walk through the door, so give yourself an ego boost before you even leave home.

'Stand in front of the mirror and think back to the last time you went out looking utterly gorgeous,' says Susan Quilliam, psychologist and author of *Body Language Secrets* (HarperCollins). 'Then adopt a "confidence pose" – put your shoulders back, keep your head held up and pull your stomach in, all of which will make you look taller and more noticeable,' she explains.

Dancing confidently is another way to reel him in – and much easier than you think, according to dance tutor Ruth Howard-Jones of London's Pineapple Dance Studios. 'Look him straight in the eye, put on your best smile and just wiggle those hips,' she says. 'Turning around and glancing at him over your shoulder as you dance is also very sexy.' You don't have to pull off any fancy moves, either – and don't look at your feet. 'Keep your head up and don't worry about what your feet are doing, because if your top half looks good, no one notices what's happening below,' explains Howard-Jones.

PURSUE-YOU RULE 4

Be Miss Popular

Skulking around in the corner with a double vodka won't make you look mysterious, just unfriendly and totally unapproachable. Enjoying yourself with a group of friends gives off the signal that you're confident, easy-going and fun to be around, all of which will make him want to get to know you better. Surrounding yourself with friends of both sexes will instantly make you appear more attractive, as it shows men find you entertaining. But while going out in a group will definitely get him interested, it's a brave man who will actually pluck up the nerve to speak to you in front of them.

*L*OVE NOTE
GENTLY WHISPER IN HIS EAR 'I LOVE YOU SOOOO MUCH' (BUT NOT IF IT'S A FIRST DATE!).

'If you go out with a group of friends or even one girlfriend, make sure you separate from them at some stage so you're more approachable,' advises Heskell. 'No man wants to be rejected in front of a group of women, and he may well feel he can't approach you when you are "protected" by a herd of friends.' What you should do is brush past him – maybe on the way to the loo and whisper 'excuse me', or make eye contact with him while you're at the bar. 'You need to give him the signal that you want him to come over, and by looking at him or touching him, he'll get the message,' says Heskell.

PURSUE-YOU RULE 5

Speak like a sex symbol
If you already have the husky tones of Mariella Frostrup, you can skip this section. If not, there are simple vixen-voice tips that will have him melting the moment you open your mouth. Firstly, a voice that always falls at the end of the sentence sounds negative and is a turn-off, so take a tip from Kylie.

'Australians have a raised inflection in their speech, so their voices go up at the end of a sentence,' says Roz Comins, coordinator of the Voice Care Network charity and a vocal trainer who works with actors. 'You shouldn't use it all the time, because you would sound silly,' she explains, 'but if you do it every so often, you'll sound more positive and interesting.'

Secondly, don't whisper in the hope that he'll move closer to hear what you're saying – according to Comins, he's more likely to give up making conversation because he'll think you're too quiet and reserved. Concentrating on how much you fancy him is also a key to attracting him because if you think sexy thoughts, they'll be echoed in your voice.

Finally, bizarre as it sounds – try and think of your 'prey' as a puppy. 'The sexiest voice is a stroking voice,' says Comins. 'Think what it's like to stroke a puppy and the way you would use your voice as you did it. So, lower your voice slightly and adopt a soothing tone as you speak – he'll love it!'

PURSUE-YOU RULE 6

Show your scentuality
The most subtle way of getting men to fall at your feet is to deploy your secret weapons: pheromones.

These are odourless chemicals your body gives off which drive the opposite sex wild with desire! The pheromones you produce are linked to your immune system – if your body is

NOEL J FEDERIZO

fighting off infection, it subtly changes the way you smell. If you're fighting fit and healthy, men will be more attracted to them, so make sure you're in peak pulling condition.

And if you want to improve on what Mother Nature gave you, there are products to help. Sensual notes in perfumes, such as jasmine and musk, are thought to mimic the body's hormones and act as powerful aphrodisiacs. Apply these to your pulse points, but avoid dabbing them behind your ears – the skin there produces an oil that changes the nature of the scent.

PURSUE-YOU RULE 7
The eyes have it
Eyes are the cornerstone of body language and the key to attracting him. 'If you're listening well, your body language is a mirror of what the other person is saying,' says Quilliam. Make eye contact to make the subliminal point that you 'click' and are worth getting to know. 'Don't worry if he looks away – he may have

to in order to think – but keep your gaze on his face,' she explains.

Glancing down and fluttering your eyelashes occasionally are classic flirt signals guaranteed to get his pulse racing. Also, when you're attracted to someone, your pupils dilate and men subconsciously pick up on that signal, too. 'While you can't consciously control your pupils, they do dilate in a dark environment,' explains Dr Bull. 'So opt for dimly lit clubs and bars. Your pupils will look huge, and by appearing attracted to the man you're after, he'll be attracted to you.'

PURSUE-YOU RULE 8
Come-to-bed come on
He's noticed you and you've been having a fabulously flirty conversation for most of the night. But how do you make sure you have him exactly where you want him?

Quilliam advises a three-step technique, starting with the 'pull back'. 'This is a slight withdrawal of all these signals, aimed to make him feel slightly insecure, to

show him what he'll be missing if he doesn't take advantage of what you are offering,' she says. Start by lowering your gaze or looking away from him. The next stage is the 'block off', to turn his attention back to you. Techniques include shifting your body so it forms a barrier between him and other people, or slipping his name into another conversation to get his attention.

Finally, go in for the kill with the 'promise' – an intimation of things to come using the power of suggestion. 'Tell him what it would be like to touch you and what it would be like to have you touch him,' says Quilliam. 'At this stage your hand may absent-mindedly stroke your face, your tongue may lick your lips...' He won't be able to join you in the cab queue fast enough. ∎

You need someone to love you, while you're looking for someone to love.

Shelagh Delaney

CAN'T FLIRT,
Won't Flirt?

No one – not even the
Sex and The City girls –
can be a full-time flirt.
But what if you just find
it impossible? Follow our
simple, guaranteed-to-
succeed guidelines and
you too can learn to flirt
with finesse.

RADIATE CONFIDENCE

'I'm useless at flirting.' say so many of us, but anyone can do it. The key is to loosen up. If someone smiles at you or raises their eyebrows at the length of the bus queue, smile back. (Basic instincts should warn you if the person is a potential maniac!) Positive human contact breeds positive self-belief, and learning to smile at strangers is a big start.

KEY POINT Realise that others genuinely want to speak to you, and smile back.

DON'T THINK ABOUT REJECTION

If you believe others won't like you, they may not. Tuning into instincts will help: if it feels right to speak to someone it probably is. Once you get to into the habit of speaking up, you'll do it more and more.

Sauce SIGNALS

Flirting is a subtle art, but even the tiniest action can say so much. We asked the body language experts how women flirt.

HOW YOU FLIRT	WHAT IT MEANS
Swaying hips, placing hands on hips	Focuses attention on your pelvis, suggesting ample capacity for child-bearing
Arching eyebrows, exaggerated facial expressions and giggling	By making your eyes appear larger, like a child's, and giggling you emphasise youth and playfulness.
Licking lips	Drawing attention to what biologists say are facial echoes of vaginal lips, transmits sexual maturity.
Averting your gaze, being coy	Playing 'hard to get' implies standards and communicates unwillingness to give yourself to 'just anyone'.

'I used to be so shy,' says flirting guru Peta Heskell. 'I'd go to discos but never speak to anyone because I was terrified of rejection. In the end, everyone just wrote me off as an ice-maiden.' Peta overcame her fear by realising it's the same for everyone and whatever you look like, if you're closed up like a clam, you'll be unapproachable.

KEY POINT Make yourself approachable by using open and relaxed body language – not hunched and defensive

GET YOUR ANTENNAE GOING

Many of us feel that if we so much as smile at a man, he's instantly going to think we want to sleep with him. That's simply not the case, and if it is, the man will soon make that obvious – and you can set him straight in no uncertain terms. We may even worry our friends will label us desperate for

I loved Kirk, so much I would have skied down Mount Everest in the nude with a carnation up my nose.

Joyce McKinney

VICTORIA RAUHOFFER

chatting to strangers. The point is, it's all about responses. Take time to read and interpret another's message. If someone isn't interested in what you say, they'll look away or find an excuse to leave. If they don't, you're on safe ground. Simply chatting is never a sign you fancy someone.

KEYPOINT Learn to recognise when someone is interested. And don't worry about what outsiders think; others are less interested in us than we realise.

SAY 'I CAN'

It's the silent, inner voice that says 'I can't...' We all have one, it's called insecurity, and sometimes it's so loud, we're terrified other people can hear it, too. Try and deafen yourself to it by learning a phrase to repeat to yourself. Something like 'I have beautiful eyes' will take your mind off your demon.

KEYPOINT Repeat that mantra in your head when the wobbles start.

LEAVE YOUR FRIENDS BEHIND

Yes, friends can be a big barrier to flirting, just by being there. Huddling in a group makes you seem unapproachable to men. Encourage your friends to be less cliquey, maybe splitting up when

you arrive at a club. 'When we go out in a group, my friends and I splinter off into twos and threes, flit about and take comfort in knowing the others are about,' says Suzy, 28, a publisher's assistant. 'We only huddle up occasionally for a big pow-wow – otherwise it's too daunting for someone to approach us.'

KEY POINT Go out in twos and threes occasionally, and try to do some activities on your own. ∎

*L*OVE NOTE

FIND SOME EXCUSE TO BEND DOWN – THE SMALLEST HINT OF CLEAVAGE OR THE MEREST GLIMPSE OF BRA WILL AWAKEN HIS LIBIDO.

NOEL J FEDERIZO

COME-AND-GET-ME
flirting TRICKS

HERE ARE COSMO'S SURE-TO-SCORE SUGGESTIONS

1 Practice 'The Look'. Stare straight at someone, look away quickly, dip your head and then look back, dropping your chin slightly. Sounds ridiculous, but really works to signal interest.

2 Sit or stand at an angle to your flirtee. Then tilt your head downwards, but look upwards towards them.

3 Always have a beautiful 'detail'. Perfect nails, a stunning necklace, a tiny henna tattoo, the latest book... people will want to know more.

4 Learn to accept compliments with grace. Thank the person who's blessed you with a positive comment like, 'Thanks, it's new,' or, 'Thanks, I'm so pleased you think so.' They'll feel clever and perceptive, and you'll feel immensely flattered. After all, claiming you actually look a wreck says nothing for the other person's taste, does it?

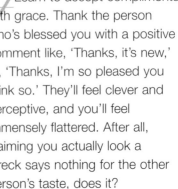

TAMARA SCHLESINGER

5 Pout slightly – but make sure you don't simply look sullen or bored to tears.

6 Drop your voice a note. Most of us speak more loudly than we need to. You'll sound instantly sexier and more attractive and he'll have to lean in to hear you. Don't shout into his ear, whisper seductively into his neck.

7 If you can hear it, blink in time with the breathing of your intended victim.

8 When looking him, imagine their face is a triangle. Move across the forehead, then down to the chin and back up to the other side. Keep the first look above the neck!

9 Clean hair, clean teeth, sweet breath and neat fingernails are great flirting assets.

10 Be clear about what you want to communicate. It's easy to get a man to sleep with you, harder to make them call. So flirt for friendship first.

11 Show interest when someone is talking. Looking over a shoulder, or changing the subject is off-putting.

12 Lick your lips...

13 Never ask a person what they do for a living, it's seen as a sign you base your judgement solely on that. Instead ask what they enjoy doing. Nine times out of ten, they'll enjoy telling you.

14 Lean in towards him, with the shoulder closest to him slightly turned down.

15 Blink slowly and flutter your eyelashes – but maintain eye contact with him.

16 Practice eye-contact with strangers so you'll be ready when you need to appear confident.

17 Touch your feet and let your shoe dangle from your foot – its supposed to mimic the muscle tension of orgasm.

18 Make little gestures as if you want to touch someone – but don't do it.

19 Have some small-talk – the last film you saw or book you read – at the ready.

20 Make one first move to speak to someone you don't know. The knock-on effects are potentially fabulous. However, if you're rejected, promise yourself you will try again another time. ■

DON'T VIE FOR HIS
Attention

Sometimes events don't go according to plan, even when you've followed all our tried-and-tested tricks to the very letter. You are merrily chatting away to him, he seems entranced and is laughing in all the right places when another woman bowls up, 'Tony/Mark/Matthew daaarrrling! How are you? Mwa! Mwa!' She tactically ignores you, gives a stiff nod when he introduces you, and proceeds to monopolise him, practically clawing at his chest.

PHAM

You have a choice. You could, of course, start a vicious verbal battle – you and she fighting for his attention, interrupting each other, shooting each other snide looks, gabbling, babbling, pawing, feeling stupid and childish – while he looks on in slightly smug amusement and thinks he's it. (In the circumstances, even Mr Right can be forgiven for this assumption.)

Well, you're not going to pander to his ego or to Mwa Mwa's need to slight every woman she regards as a threat. It reduces you to beggar status – 'Oh pleeeeze choose meee' – it is undignified and you're better than that.

The smart woman cuts in within, say, two minutes of Mwa Mwa's arrival, says loudly, 'Tony/Mark/Matthew, lovely to meet you but there are a million people I should say hello to – say goodbye to me before you go,' and leans forward to kiss him while accidentally on purpose treading heavily on Mwa Mwa's toe. Then she swans off. Walking away doesn't mean you're giving up. It shows him that you rate yourself, and you're not just there for the taking.

It also shows your contempt for Mwa Mwa and highlights the fact that she is a pretty shallow waste of space. Mwa Mwa has novelty value – she's cute enough to flit around, talk entertaining nonsense, and flirt wildly – but dig deeper and she has nothing terribly interesting to say and, in truth, Mr Right finds her a bit much.

Five minutes after you've gone he'll be missing you. If he was interested, your 'If you want me come and get me' behaviour will have stoked that interest – men still love a challenge. Ten minutes later, he will probably unpick Mwa Mwa's claws from his arm and come looking for you.

TRUTH NOTES

● It has to be said that on rare occasions, after you've walked off, he and Mwa Mwa kiss passionately and go home together. In which case the man has truly terrible taste, but – and but is all that can be salvaged from the situation – at least you preserved your dignity. If he really wanted you, he would have shaken off Mwa Mwa and come and found you. By sticking to him like an agoraphobic leech you would not have won him. He knew who he preferred at the start of the evening and no amount of vying would have changed his mind. You would merely have made yourself feel foolish as it became obvious to all and sundry that he preferred Mwa Mwa to you. You lost nothing.

● Ideally, when Mwa Mwa tries to butt in, Mr Right will make it clear by his body language (touching you on the arm, looking at you when he speaks, asking you what you think) that he will not stand any rudeness from her because he likes you and, very likely, prefers you.

● However, even the sweetest man can be so awed by the attentions of two females (a common male fantasy, as if you didn't know) that he just wants to sit back and let them claw it out. Which is why the point above is a relatively rare occurrence. ∎

QUIZ

IS HE WORTHY OF YOUR LOVE?

Find out whether your man's worthy to worship at the temple of you, is not fit to paint your fingernails, or is just in need of a little TLC (Tender Loving Changing).

ADAM OLSZEWSKI

1 You're dressed up to the nines for a meeting. His reaction when he sees you:

a 'Hey, can I be around when you take those clothes off? '
b He doesn't say anything.
c 'You look nice today.'

2 The boss came down really hard on you at work. Shaken, you feel like crawling into bed and staying there for a week. You call your honey to weep and whine. He:

a Listens sympathetically, then offers to come over and snuggle. Brings a tub of ice cream.
b Cuts the conversation short – he's meeting the guys for beers.
c Listens, suggests you get a good night's sleep, and calls you the next day to check how you are.

3 He makes sure you climax:

a When he does or soon thereafter.
b Before he does.
c You're on your own there, kid.

4 Out of nowhere, you start getting anxiety attacks. Your boyfriend:

a Helps you hunt down a therapist.
b Tells you it's all in your head.
c Shows concern but seems a little freaked by your behaviour.

5 You're out to dinner, and when the bill arrives, your boyfriend:

a Lets you know your portion of the bill, pointing out that you ordered two glasses of wine plus an appetizer salad while he only had a beer and burger.
b Says, 'It would be my pleasure' when you reach for your wallet.
c Puts down cash for half the amount.

6 When a gorgeous woman walks by both of you, he usually:

a Sneaks a sideways look at her.
b Stares at her long and hard.

c Says, 'Don't worry, darling, she's not even fit to polish your pumps!'

7 When the two of you have a fight, you end up feeling:

a Frustrated. He shuts down.
b As if you are in the process of working something out. He may get mad, but he always remains rational.
c Frightened by his behaviour.

8 You tell your boyfriend that your mum/sister/girlfriend has just advised you against taking that fabulous new job. His response:

a 'Don't listen to her, you'll be great.'
b 'She's just afraid for you. You'll be great.'
c 'I never really liked your mum.'

9 You had a terrific time at the party – sure, you flirted with a couple of men, but it

was all in good fun. The next day, your boyfriend would most likely:

a Be turned on by your popularity.
b Amorously tell you how lucky he is to be the one who goes home with you.
c Sulk and make a snide comment about your drinking.

10 When both of you spend a weekend together:

a You often feel lonely; he sits in front of the TV a lot, tinkers in the garage.
b You're completely comfortable – you both laugh, relax, make love.
c The sex is fabulous, though he's lazy about making out-of-bed plans.

11 How do your friends describe the man you are dating?

a The catch of the year.
b A nice man who seems to adore you.
c Someone to have fun with but not someone you want to get serious with.

12 Tick any of the following statements that apply:

a When he knows something (a fact or current event) you don't know, he never patronises you.

b He would get allergy shots so he could live with you and your two cats.

c He's tried to turn you on to whatever sport he's into (golf, kayaking, baseball).

d You frequently hear from friends that he's been bragging about you.

e He truly doesn't even notice when you've put on an extra 5 pounds.

f He brings home unexpected treats for you – CDs of groups you've said you like, articles he's cut out that would interest you, your favourite cookies.

g He doesn't freak when you cry or accuse you of having PMT.

h He holds hands and hugs a lot – always makes you feel cherished.

i If he found a wallet full of money, he'd hunt down the owner and give it back.

j You are comfortable with the amount of alcohol that he drinks.

SCORING

	a	b	c
1	a-3	b-1	c-2
2	a-3	b-1	c-2
3	a-2	b-3	c-1
4	a-3	b-1	c-2
5	a-1	b-3	c-2
6	a-2	b-1	c-3
7	a-2	b-3	c-1
8	a-2	b-3	c-1
9	a-2	b-3	c-1
10	a-1	b-3	c-2
11	a-3	b-2	c-1

12 Give yourself 3 points for each statement ticked.

MORE THAN 44 POINTS: Worthy

'A worthy man is one who makes you feel good when you are around him,' says psychologist Michele Kasson, co-author of *The Men Out There* (Rutledge).

'The two of you have shared goals and common interests, and you each give the other support in facing the tough, cruel world.' He's kind, compassionate, supportive... but not just to you. 'If he treats his mum – and even the waiter – well,' adds Kasson, 'then he will be respectful of you too.' Remember, though, true love doesn't mean conflict-free love. How do you handle the situation when problems arise? 'Do you feel more connected and like you know each other better after a disagreement?' asks Daphne Rose Kingma, author of *Coming Apart* (Conari Press). 'Couples who are not threatened by differences but instead see them as a process of discovery have wonderful relationships.'

26 TO 44 POINTS: Workable

Every man has his good points... and his flaws. The question is, can you live with this man's imperfections – can you even get him to change some annoying behaviour?

'We all have a bottom line when it comes to choosing another human being to love,' says Kingma. 'A woman needs to ask herself, "Does this man have the one quality that is most important to me in a mate?" It may be that he shares your spiritual values or is willing to communicate. This is the grounding bond that, over time, allows the various imperfections of your relationship to recede.'

In addition, we all have a number of qualities we'd prefer to have in a relationship. Kingma suggests you make a list of ten characteristics that you would like your man to have. If he has five, it's probably worth sticking around. 'Also, see how he responds to the fact that he has attributes you dislike,' adds Kingma. 'He may be a football fanatic; perhaps you can convince him to watch at a pal's house so you can have the place to yourself.'

Also, remember what's truly important to you. 'Forgetting the anniversary of your first date is chump change,' says Sharyn Wolf, author of *How to Stay Lovers for Life* (Dutton). 'You want to be with the guy who'll sit with you in the doctor's surgery if you find a lump in your breast.'

If there is some aspect of his behaviour that you truly can't put up with, then approach changing him in a positive way. 'You can only change a man who wants to change,' says Kingma. 'But he has to be inspired by love, not nagging. For example, if you're a health nut and he expresses a desire to get in shape, you can be supportive of him, but if six months pass and it hasn't happened, then you've got to decide whether or not you can live with this in the long run.'

FEWER THAN 26 POINTS: Worthless

This man dismisses your feelings, has more fun channel-surfing than talking with you, and ogles other women right in front of you. Are you so eager to be with a man – any man – that you will settle for someone clearly so undeserving of your love?

'You simply can't be with someone who has more emotional power in the relationship than you do,' says Kasson. 'If you feel you can't stand up for yourself, then this isn't the right man for you.'

Perhaps you're aware that you're stuck in an unhealthy relationship – so why is it so hard for you to leave? 'Because we all want to be loved and we're afraid no one else will come along again,' says Kingma. 'But the truth is, every person I've ever counselled who's ended a relationship has found someone better.' If you know you need to leave him and you can't do it on your own, ask trusted friends for their support or even get some help from a professional counsellor.

*It's strong and it's sudden
It could be cruel
sometimes
But it might just save your life.
That's the power of love.*
Colla/Hayes/Lewis, as sung by Huey Lewis and the News

Love is the best of opiates.
Stevie Smith

10 SIGNS HE'S THE ONE

1 He spends the weekend with your family and still wants to date you.

2 When you argue with him, he never puts it down to your PMT.

3 He lets you use his toothbrush when you crash at his place.

4 He doesn't fall asleep immediately after sex.

5 He looks at Pamela Anderson centrefolds and insists he doesn't know what the big deal is.

6 On FA Cup Final day, he offers to spend the day in bed, painting your toenails and giving you backrubs.

7 He leaves you cute little 'shmoopie' messages every day at work... and has for the past 2 years.

8 Even after seeing you in a mud mask stuffing your face with Ben & Jerry's, he still looks at you the same way he did the moment he first saw you.

9 He brings you your favourite daisies just because it's Tuesday.

10 He insists on waking up at 5 a.m. just to take you to the airport.

THE MOMENT I KNEW HE WASN'T WORTHY

'My father died, and my boyfriend told me he was "sorry but couldn't handle it" and promptly disappeared for the next few weeks.'
Tina, 29

'He asked me not to tell his ultraconservative friends that I volunteer at Planned Parenthood.'
Linda, 28

'He didn't understand why my sister was angry that her husband went golfing the day she had their baby.'
Valerie, 24

'He bought the Sunday papers and then said, "Can I have £3.50, because I won't have time to read them." I knew he was cheap, but that really was the final straw.'
Suzanne, 31

LOVE NOTE
SURROUND YOURSELVES WITH 50 TEALIGHTS, COVER HIM WITH BODY GLITTER AND HAVE SPARKLY SEX.

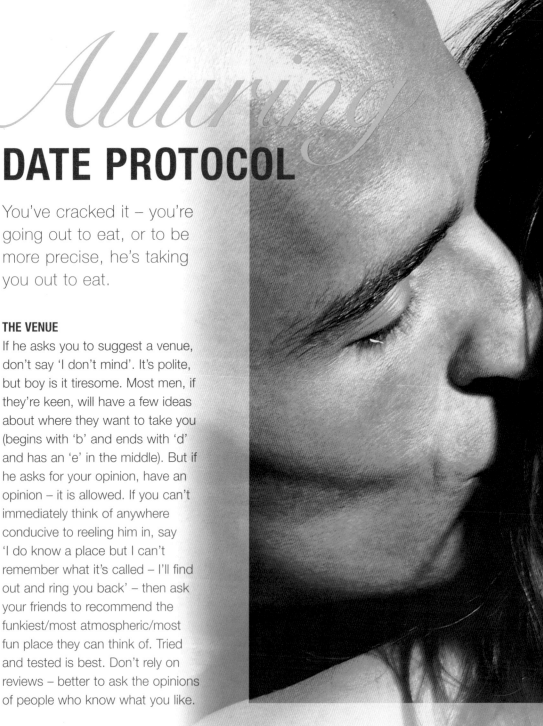

Alluring
DATE PROTOCOL

You've cracked it – you're going out to eat, or to be more precise, he's taking you out to eat.

THE VENUE

If he asks you to suggest a venue, don't say 'I don't mind'. It's polite, but boy is it tiresome. Most men, if they're keen, will have a few ideas about where they want to take you (begins with 'b' and ends with 'd' and has an 'e' in the middle). But if he asks for your opinion, have an opinion – it is allowed. If you can't immediately think of anywhere conducive to reeling him in, say 'I do know a place but I can't remember what it's called – I'll find out and ring you back' – then ask your friends to recommend the funkiest/most atmospheric/most fun place they can think of. Tried and tested is best. Don't rely on reviews – better to ask the opinions of people who know what you like.

SERGIO DE DIMITIIS

It's best not to choose somewhere impossibly posh or 'romantic' – the contrived atmosphere is pressurising at the least, excruciating at the most. It makes both of you uncomfortably self-conscious, and dammit, you don't want to be on your best behaviour. Better somewhere loud, reasonably raucous, where you can relax, enjoy yourselves, laugh loudly without the entire restaurant turning to stare, and get into a juicy conversation without being bothered by the waiter sweeping the table with a silly little brush.

THE FOOD

Eat – normal men like women with a healthy appetite. A woman who eats like an anorexic sparrow, who picks at her mixed salad (no dressing) like it's poisoned, refuses dessert and pats her flat-as-an-ironing-board stomach and says 'Phew, I'm stuffed' is – as far as her date can see – a liar, liar, pants on fire.

Women who see some strange virtue in starving themselves may, occasionally, stoke a man's paternal instinct – he'll want to feed you up and protect you because you're obviously such a damn fool you won't eat enough without being nagged. But men who are very attracted by a woman who starves herself (entirely different, of

course, to a woman who's naturally skinny) are, to be frank, odd. An attitude like that betrays a curious view of women – as if he thinks they should be small and weak. A man who feels distaste for a woman who can eat two Big Macs, then say 'Where's the apple pie?' has problems.

I'll jump to the conclusion that he is threatened by strong women. Which is to say, a good, sexy man – a man worth seducing – is far more likely to go for you if you eat like a normal human being. Think *Nine and a Half Weeks*. Food is sexy, watching a woman eat is sexy. This isn't to say you should everything on the menu to the point where you feel nauseous and your trouser button pops. But have fun with your food.

ORDER SOMETHING SEXY

You can either be brazen and order oysters – hmmm – possibly too blatant, but if you're flirting outrageously at this stage, go for it. You don't however, want him to think you're snarfing as many extortionate delicacies as you can stuff at his expense, so say something like 'We'll go halves' – a nicely ambiguous statement, but also see below for paying protocol. Mussels (used by magazine editors everywhere to illustrate features on the vagina!) are, providing they're

NORMAL MEN LIKE WOMEN WITH A HEALTHY APPETITE. FOOD IS SEXY, AND WATCHING A WOMAN EAT IS SEXY.

fresh, less expensive and less obvious, but just as saucy. The idea is to get him thinking about sex any devious way you can.

Spaghetti is good because it's slithery and you can suck it up (he may think 'blow job') – although admittedly, if you splatter tomato sauce all over your face and top at the same time, he may just think 'messy eater'. To be on the safe side, choose a spaghetti dish with lemon and butter and herbs so if it does splatter a little, it won't make you look like he can't take you anywhere.

PINCHING HIS FOOD

Pinching food off his plate is cute, but not that cute. If you ask him for a chip, that's his cue to feed you one. But don't hint: 'Ooh, those chips look nice. I wish I'd ordered some,' and grab a bunch off his plate. Men are territorial about their food. They don't like people pinching it. Also, he probably has a back catalogue of ex-girlfriends who never ordered their own dessert, but scooped up two-thirds of his so fast their arms nearly popped out of their sockets – ie it conjures up bad memories – he wishes you'd just order your own, and it frustrates him that

you didn't. He doesn't understand the logic behind the fact that some women feel the calories don't count if they come off someone else's plate. And even if he did, he'd just think it's daft.

Yet, you can have fun with each other's food. Ask him if he wants to taste yours (rude pun intended) and if he does and then hesitates, scoop up a little on your fork and feed it to him. If he scoops up some of your food with his own fork, or looks as if he is about to, he's missed (you judge whether accidentally or not) a supreme flirting opportunity and can best be described as a goober.

WHO PAYS?

If he asks you out on a first date, courtesy demands that he pays. Nothing to do with sexism – it's the same if you ask a client to join you for lunch, you pay. (Of course, if you ask your mother to join you for coffee, she pays – but she's the exception that proves the rule.)

However, it is not nice to assume. You are a modern, independent woman, not a spoiled brat, and courtesy also demands that you offer to pay. You don't have to offer to pay the entire bill – although if it's been a blast, why not – but he'll appreciate it if you

*L*OVE NOTE

SEX BURNS CALORIES! SO THE MORE YOU HAVE IT, THE MORE TONED YOU BECOME AND THE MORE CONFIDENT YOU FEEL IN BED.

suggest making a contribution. As he gets out his plastic, reach for your bag and say 'Let me help you with that.' This is the test. Either he says:

● 'Absolutely not. How dare you. Put that away.' (Steady dear, it's a purse, not a gun. Suggests he's a tad conservative and thinks ladies should never pay for their own dinners. A double-edged sword, this one, because he'll also think, I'll be bound, that ladies should have long shiny hair right down to their bottoms.)

● 'No, please, let me.' (Polite, well-mannered, but no indication of whether he feels pleased or merely obliged.)

● 'This is my shout! You can pay next time.' (Healthy, sweet-natured man! Also telling you quite plainly he's keen to meet up again. Excellent, meriting a gold star.)

● 'Are you sure? Well, if you insist.' (Cheapskate.)

Or he tots up the bill, working out precisely what you both owe. (In which case pay what you owe, then bid him a cold goodnight and never see him again.)

If he flips when you offer to help pay, the sweet thing to do is to say 'Are you sure? Well, thank you very much.'

If he coolly insists on paying, the sweet thing to do is also to say 'Are you sure? Well, thank you very

IF HE SUGGESTS YOU PAY NEXT TIME, TREAT HIM TO YOUR MOST DEVASTATING SMILE AND LET HIM KNOW THAT YOU TOO ARE KEEN TO MEET UP AGAIN.

much.' There's no need to launch into a great palaver of 'Are you sure you're sure… no really… are you really sure, bore bore.' He's said he'd like to pay, you questioned him once, he's reassured you, fine. That's it. You'll take his word for it, you're both adults conversing like adults, you'll believe him – you haven't got time to play word games all night.

ANNOYANCE NOTE

However, it has been known for a man to respond at this point 'You didn't put up much of a fight!' To which you archly reply 'Was I supposed to?'

If he suggests you pay next time – assuming you want there to be a next time – you treat him to your most devastating smile and say 'Thank you very much, I will pay next time.' Thus, you graciously accept and you let him know you too are keen to meet up again.

If he lets you pay half, either he is desperately, desperately short of cash (in which case he would have been wise to suggest a cheap but funky venue) or – and this is more probable – he isn't as mad keen as we thought. He's also mildly rude. Let it pass, but to be frank, it doesn't bode brilliantly. If he totals up exactly what you owe, write him off. Now. ■

*Of all forms of caution, caution in love is
perhaps the most fatal to true happiness.*

Bertrand Russell

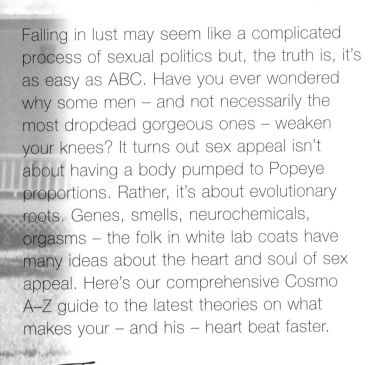

Falling in lust may seem like a complicated process of sexual politics but, the truth is, it's as easy as ABC. Have you ever wondered why some men – and not necessarily the most dropdead gorgeous ones – weaken your knees? It turns out sex appeal isn't about having a body pumped to Popeye proportions. Rather, it's about evolutionary roots. Genes, smells, neurochemicals, orgasms – the folk in white lab coats have many ideas about the heart and soul of sex appeal. Here's our comprehensive Cosmo A–Z guide to the latest theories on what makes your – and his – heart beat faster.

'I want to MAKE LOVE to You'

THE A TO BED OF ATTRACTION

RK BARRETT

As soon as I wake up
Every night
Every day
I know that it's you I need
To take the blues away
It must be love, love, love
It must be love, love, love.

Labi Siffre, as sung by Madness

_A_ IS FOR AVERAGE

The big surprise of modern science (not to mention modern love) is that our notion of what's beautiful is... what's average. Studies show that, from England to Australia, the ideal of attractiveness is very middle of the road. A study at Texas University took 32 female faces and, using computers, averaged all their features into composite shots of each face. When shown the full display, both men and women picked the synthesised versions as most attractive.

This individuality-is-less-attractive theory springs from a prehistoric instinct that the more average a person is, the less likely they are to suffer from health problems that will be passed on to their offspring.

Besides this, average is unthreatening. Face it, however lust-worthy you think Antonio Banderas is, you're going to feel far more secure in a relationship with someone who doesn't inspire every woman he meets to drool at his feet.

_B_ IS FOR BASIC INSTINCT

According to biologists, we only play the mating game to hand down our genes. Dr David Buss, professor of psychology at Michigan University and author of

HOWEVER LUST-WORTHY YOU THINK ANTONIO BANDERAS IS, YOU'LL FEEL MORE SECURE WITH A MAN WHO DOESN'T INSPIRE EVERY WOMAN HE MEETS TO FALL AT HIS FEET.

The Evolution Of Desire: Strategies Of Human Mating (Basic), looked at more than 10,000 people of all ages in 37 countries and says he found men are suckers for anything young (we needed a study for this?). He explains, 'For males, attraction is a lot like a medical check-list: youth, shiny hair without grey, good teeth, clear, smooth skin. In biological terms, this adds up to a physical inventory indicating the female is in the peak of her childbearing years.'

The woman, however, doesn't just fall for the first sperm paddling past. She requires something a bit more practical, such as food and protection. Why? Because the female invests far more time and energy in reproduction and child-rearing and wants an assurance of some kind that the guy is up to the job – at least in terms of child-support payments.

Which explains why Dr Buss found the way a man dresses, rather than his age, is the most important factor for a woman. 'Universally, women are attracted to somewhat older, well-dressed men because those attributes are clues to resources and status,' he says. Surely not! 'Put a suit and a Rolex on a man and see how well he fares next to his identical twin in a Burger King hat.' Well, when you put it like that...

$\mathcal{C}$ IS FOR CUTENESS, NOT CHARACTER

Love may be foolish but, in fact, it's never blind. People are first attracted to each other not because their object of desire has all the gentle qualities of Gandhi or Mother Theresa, but rather because they look nothing like Gandhi or Mother Theresa.

According to a long-running nationwide survey of male and female sex appeal, a woman's looks matter far more at first glance to a man than vice versa. Psychologist Dr Victor Johnston tracked down beauty preferences using a computer programme called FacePrints. People rate the images of men and women, the computer then 'breeds' the top 10 faces to create two digital offspring that replace the lowest-rated faces. After a few rounds, you end up with a perfect 10.

Dr Johnston discovered the preferred look for women is higher forehead than average, fuller lips, smaller chin and nose, and fairly prominent eyes and cheekbones. In fact, the ideal 25-year-old woman his team pieced together in 1993 had the facial characteristics of a Barbie doll.

Women aren't immune to the appearance lure. We're just not looking for a prepubescent romp. According to the FacePrints study,

ACCORDING TO THE EXPERTS, WE ARE MORE OFTEN ATTRACTED TO SOMEONE WE HAVE TO CHASE THAN TO SOMEONE WHO'S MORE READILY AVAILABLE.

what generally turns our heads is tall, dark and older, with a square jaw, strong chin, Roman nose and bushy eyebrows. Elvis lives!

 IS FOR DAZZLING

It turns out merely looking at certain bright colours can make us physically hot, speeding up our breathing and heart rates. In one university study, both men and women rated red as the most erotic colour, followed by dark blue, violet and black. The only hue the sexes disagreed over was green – women found it sexy and men didn't. Virginal white didn't even get a look-in.

$\mathcal{E}$ IS FOR EQUALITY

This is a marketplace concept of love. Named the equity principle, by psychologist Dr Elaine Hatfield, the idea is you only fall for someone you think will give about the same amount as you, or, in plain English, you're likely to fall for someone who is on a par with you looks or career-wise, because otherwise it disrupts the power balance in the relationship, making you feel either totally in control or very inadequate. That's why beautiful people usually attract beautiful people. Shame – some of those genes really ought to be spread about a bit.

𝓕 IS FOR FLESH AND BLOOD

Have you ever wondered why you're drawn into romantic entanglements with men you shouldn't even consider having coffee with? The reason: imprinting. We click with certain people because they invoke our earliest memories.

'My experience as a couples therapist has convinced me that people tend to be attracted to replicas of their parents or siblings,' explains Dr David Pearson, a US clinical psychologist. 'On a subconscious level, we fall in love with people who remind us of people we loved when we were small. Hopefully, they will nurture us like Mum or Dad did – only better. By recreating the environment of childhood, we hope to heal the psychological damage we all experienced to some degree when we were young, no matter how many happy memories we may have.'

How's that for a totally mind-blowing concept? After years of trying to avoid becoming anything like our parents, we now attempt to date them. 'There's often a strong family resemblance as well,' adds Dr Pearson. Which explains just why some couples can pass for siblings.

𝓛OVE NOTE
USE SCENTED CANDLES TO ENHANCE THE MOOD: VANILLA TO AROUSE OR ORANGE TO EXCITE.

𝓖 IS FOR GENITAL ECHO

According to anthropologist Desmond Morris, this alluring term covers body parts with a passing resemblance to a love organ – in other words, a visual sexual double entendre. The belly button is one example, the fingers another (you work out the matching genitals). But the mother of all echoes is the mouth, considered to be a dead ringer for the vagina. In the same way the inner labia of the vagina redden with engorged blood just prior to orgasm, so our lips also become redder when we're turned on. Which is probably why bright red lipstick is thought to be such a strong sexual signal and why glossy lips simulate vaginal lubrication.

Then there's the kiss itself. 'Pressing lips is considered to be such an intimate act that few prostitutes do it,' says 'William Cane, author of The Book Of Kisses (Robert Hale Publishers). As Julia Roberts said in Pretty Woman, 'It's too personal.'

𝓗 IS FOR HOT PURSUIT

Apparently, we are more often attracted to someone we have to chase than someone who's more readily available. 'Having an urge frustrated can intensify the feeling of need,' speculates psychologist Dr Janet Klein, 'making us interpret it as a must-have desire.'

I IS FOR IMITATION

Hang out at a party, pub or any social arena where the sexes mix and you'll see a lot of copycat body talk. 'It's called mirroring,' explains body-language consultant Dr Anna Gooden. 'When two people become captivated with each other, they begin to subtly and unconsciously mimic each other's postures and gestures.'

The first clue that attraction is in the air is when the wannabe lovers rotate until they're standing face to face, with feet, knees, hands, shoulders or whole bodies pointing towards each other. They move in perfect rhythm, all the while gazing into each other's eyes. If he crosses his legs, she crosses hers. If she leans forward, so does he.

J IS FOR JUST RIGHT

It seems humans, like most other species, show a strong preference for individuals who, when you draw a line down the centre of their face, from their forehead to their chin, match up perfectly on the left and the right sides. Denzel Washington has it. Lyle Lovett, on the other

THE FIRST CLUE THAT ATTRACTION IS IN THE AIR IS WHEN WANNABE LOVERS ROTATE UNTIL THEY'RE STANDING WITH THEIR BODIES FACING TOWARDS EACH OTHER.

hand, is an asymmetrical nightmare. In fact, the computer geeks have worked out precise measurements for the perfectly symmetrical face: each eye is one-fourteenth as high as the face and three-tenths its width, the distance from the middle of the eye to the eyebrow is one-tenth the height of the face and the nose occupies no more than five per cent of the face.

And – wouldn't you know it? – these same well-balanced babes have more and better sex than their lopsided counterparts. They're even more likely to have synchronised orgasms. Biologist Dr Randy Thornhill, who conducted the study, thinks simultaneous female-male orgasm aids the sperms' journey to the egg. Otherwise, what would be the biological advantage of climaxing with a perfectly balanced man? Apart from the obvious.

'Symmetry may enhance appearance, but it isn't really about beauty,' says Dr Thornhill. It turns out symmetry suggests a strong immune system, a nourishing diet and vigorous baby-making powers to our prehistoric brains. These are all qualities our knuckle-dragging ancestors would have wanted to introduce to the reproductive family tree, while a crooked jaw or drooping eyelid indicates the possibility of a to-be-avoided-at-all-costs physical problem.

RK BARRETT

𝒦 IS FOR KNOWING INSTANTLY

'The first four minutes of visual contact between potential lovers are critical,' explains Dr Gooden. 'This is when we make up our minds about each other's physical appearance, body shape, age, status, race and, of course, sex. Posture and facial expressions help complete the picture by giving an indication of mood and personality.'

It is all accomplished with the face scan, a glance that also takes in your whole body. 'After a head-to-toe sweep, your eyes flick between the other person's eyes, move down to the mouth and finish with a few wider skims that take in the hair,' says Dr Gooden. 'If the scan lasts more than three seconds, you'll experience some sort of emotional arousal.' Much longer than that and all you'll feel is intimidation.

During the face scan, you experience what Dr Gooden refers to as the eyebrow flash – the brows automatically move up and down. 'This instantly recognised non-verbal gesture of friendly greeting is practised worldwide,' she says. 'Because it's universal, it's probably an inborn sexual response – as the eyebrows rise, the eyeballs are exposed, allowing more light onto the surface. This immediately makes them appear large, bright and attractive.'

ℒ IS FOR LOVE MAP

It's love at first sight! You lock eyes with some gorgeous stranger and zap! This man seems to fulfil all your love requirements to the last detail. But the truth behind this phenomenon is less romantic than it seems. Our heart beats faster less because of how he looks than what he reminds us of. Sexologist Dr John Money terms this our love map – the qualities that add up to our ideal partner or type.

Children develop these love maps, Dr Money thinks, between the ages of five and eight in response to bonds formed with family and friends, as well as other experiences and chance associations. So, by puberty, you have already subconsciously constructed a specific CV of your ideal partner. For any kind of zap! to occur you have to subconsciously recognise this person fits your guidelines. While no lover is a perfect match, perhaps his gaze somehow reminds you of your father's, or he wears the same aftershave as your favourite uncle...

Unfortunately, a love-map match doesn't always end happily. 'Some people find themselves drawn to the same destructive characters time and time again,' explains Dr Paula Eidelman, a clinical psychologist. 'This may be the result of what is called a repetition compulsion – a need to resolve unfinished emotional business. They may be attracted to someone who looks or acts like a person who harmed them in their early years. They are still trying to rewrite and correct the past,' explains Eidelman.

$\mathcal{M}$ IS FOR MMM – ORGASM

It took a team of scientists to confirm we're more likely to remain attracted to a sex stud than a love dud. A study conducted at Manchester University indicates the female orgasm has a bond-forming purpose. When a woman collapses in a joyful heap, her brain's levels of oxytocin (a sort of hormonal super-glue) rise, making her feel more attracted and attached to her lover. But it doesn't work the other way round, unfortunately – the degree of a woman's romantic attachment has absolutely no effect whatsoever on her orgasm.

$\mathcal{N}$ IS FOR NOISE APPRECIATION

Tchaikovsky meets Iron Maiden! A recent study of 239 students revealed our musical tastes can influence how hot we think

someone is. In the study, the men were more attracted to women with a taste for classical music, while the men's desirability was noticeably amplified by a passion for heavy metal.

$\mathcal{O}$ IS FOR OPPOSITES

There's nothing like someone diametrically opposed to us to ignite the flames of passion. 'It's the complementary theory of love,' explains Dr Eidelman. 'Sometimes we're attracted to potential mates who we perceive to be our "better half" because they have certain qualities we desire in ourselves. In forming a bond with this person, we annex those qualities and become complete.'

Yet, our perceptions may change. 'Eventually, when our own repressed feelings are stirred, we are uncomfortable and criticise our partners for being too bold, or whatever the quality was that caught our eye in the first place,' reveals Dr Eidelman. 'The characteristic that initially attracted us now repels.' But this reversal of feelings only applies with positive qualities – if you think someone is slime when you meet him, he probably is.

$\mathcal{L}$OVE NOTE

SURPRISE HIM BY HAVING A CRACKLING FIRE AND A BOTTLE OF CHILLED CHAMPAGNE READY FOR WHEN HE COMES HOME.

𝒫 IS FOR PAMELA ANDERSON

Or anyone with features somewhat larger than average. Rewind for a moment to the synthesised photo experiment that concluded average was best in terms of attraction (as in 'A is for average' on page 95), Well, back at the computer terminal, a different group of psychologists based in Scotland and Japan put together their own computer-generated Mr and Ms Average and 'enhanced' them. Her eyes, lips and cheekbones were exaggerated, while the males were given a broader jaw and brow and a more rugged complexion.

Surprise – the new improved models were perceived to be the most desirable. This supports the notion that human beings, like other animals, have evolved mechanisms to help them judge the desirability of potential mates. So, larger than average is a courtship display – a way of standing out from the crowd.

𝒬 IS FOR QUANTUM LEAP

So much for fate. Although it's not socially acceptable to say, 'I got involved because I was ready,' it seems attraction is often a matter of mental timing. Research shows most of us tend to date only between one and four people seriously before saying 'I do'.

MOST OF US TEND TO DATE ONLY BETWEEN ONE AND FOUR PEOPLE SERIOUSLY BEFORE SAYING 'I DO'.

ℛ IS FOR RANDY SEASON

It seems our bodies are more lusty during some months than others. After scrutinising birth records from around the world, German researchers concluded there's a definite human mating season.

They found chances for conception increase during the months when the sun shines for around 12 hours a day and the temperature hovers between 10°C and 21°C (this is usually mid-March to mid-September in Europe). Which means, biologically, we're more likely to look good to the opposite sex during these times of the year.

𝒮 IS FOR SOUL MATES

Similarity breeds content. As a rule, like tends to be attracted to like – individuals prefer others of the same ethnic group, with similar attitudes, interests, histories, IQs, tastes in music, religions, customs, and even physical traits like height and hair colour. In fact, research reveals this 'mutuality' may be the most important ingredient in any successful relationship.

Professor David Olson, who specialises in family social sciences, claims it's possible to predict whether a marriage will end in divorce on the very day a couple becomes engaged.

After questioning 164 courting couples on their values, Professor Olson identified more than 100 as seriously mismatched in terms of mutuality. Three years later, he interviewed the couples again and discovered 90 per cent of these lovebirds hadn't been able to make a go of it – 52 called off the wedding, 31 who'd married had already split up, and another 22 described their union as 'unhappy'. However, the remaining couples, who qualified as kindred spirits, had happily settled down to wedded bliss.

T IS FOR TWO-WAY ATTRACTION

Being attracted to someone is like taking a crash course in self-confidence. Truth is, we're more likely to be attracted to someone who is obviously attracted to us. This give-and-take element was confirmed in a university study of passion influences, where the perception of being liked ranked just as high as the presence of sex appeal in the potential partner.

Commenting on the findings of this study, psychologist Dr Arthur Afon confirms, 'The combination of the two appears to be very important. In fact, love may just not be possible without it.' So, if you like him and you know it, clap your hands.

U IS FOR UNKNOWN

Forget about the boy next door. A little mystery is essential to infatuation. People almost never become captivated by someone they know well – as a recent study on Israeli kibbutz marriages clearly illustrates. It found that out of 2,769 marriages, none occurred between men and women who had grown up together on the kibbutz. The reason? The easy familiarity of having spent their whole lives together was unconsciously translated into a chaste sibling bond instead of a passionate sexual one.

V IS FOR VITAL STATISTICS

Slim or round – which body shape do you prefer? Ask that question in mixed company and, like Dr April Fallon, a psychologist at the Medical College of Pennsylvania, you'll find it's not the men who prefer Kate Moss – it's the women. Men tend to plump for the fuller-figured model.

'If a woman is a stone over her ideal weight, it doesn't have a big impact on a man's interest level,' says Dr Fallon. What guys are attracted by, regardless of weight, is a woman with hips roughly one-third larger than her waist. Figuratively speaking, hourglass curves. In a study of Playboy

BETH STUDENBERS

*Love is its own aphrodisiac and is
the main ingredient for lasting sex.*
Mort Katz

bunnies conducted by evolutionary psychologist Professor Devendra Singh, it was found that while the curvaceous pin-up's weight has dropped by 30 per cent over the past three decades, her waist-to-hip ratio has nonetheless remained steady. Professor Singh concludes this ratio broadcasts a female's health and readiness to breed.

Meanwhile, most men think women drool over Chippendale-style muscles. However, according to recent research, the preferred shape is the 'V-shaped man', boasting slim legs, middling to thin lower trunk and middling to broad upper trunk.

W IS FOR WIN BY A NOSE

It's common knowledge that monkeys, mice and moths produce pheromones – airborne chemicals – as a kind of 'Come and get me' aromatic signal to the opposite sex. Scientists assumed humans had either never developed the ability to communicate through scent or had evolved beyond it. That is, until Thomas Getchell, an American neuroscientist, peeked up a bunch of schnozzes (it's a tough job but someone's got to do it) and discovered the vomero-nasal organ, which is the piece of nasal equipment that responds to pheromones, actually works.

'IT'S SO HOT' CAN SOUND SULTRY WHEN BREATHED IN A CANDYFLOSS WHISPER, BUT LIKE A WEATHER REPORT WHEN UTTERED IN THE TONE OF MICHAEL FISH.

Next, Claus Wedekind, a psychologist at Bern University, Switzerland, ran sniff tests to discover what makes one person's scent attractive and another's a total turn-off. He asked 49 women to sniff sweaty T-shirts worn for two days by 44 non-showering, non-deodorised, garlic-avoiding guys (all in the name of science) and rate the smells on pleasantness and sexiness. While there's no evidence pheromones have any real powers of seduction (sweaty T-shirts did not make the women amorous), it was discovered that the merest whiff of someone's scent can put the smeller in the mood for romance.

Which is probably why sweat is used as a love potion in some cultures. An old Caribbean recipe reads, 'Prepare hamburger patty. Steep in your own sweat. Cook. Serve to the person desired.' Hmm. Perhaps this isn't a seduction trick to be recommended...

X IS FOR X FACTOR

Chemistry – that magnetic sense that this person is it – isn't just meaningless lovers' talk. From the moment you feel that rush of head-over-heels lust, it's chemical warfare. When we're attracted to someone, many chemicals and hormones are released that literally gush into our body. First out of the gate is dehydroepiandrosterone, often called the mother lode because so many of our sex hormones are derived from it. In essence, it tells you who you can and can't have sex with by stimulating your sex appeal and, if it gets that far, your orgasms.

Testosterone also plays a role, acting as a potent aphrodisiac for both sexes, as does dopamine. But the main role of this sex hormone is more on the desire side, giving it a gotta-have-it edge that makes us anticipate the warm pleasure of being sexually involved.

Oestrogen is the stuff that helps make us feel more receptive to being chatted up. And when we're actually attracted to someone, the brain drenches itself in phenylethylamine, a chemical that turns our senses into a mush of passionate excitement.

But what finally clinches your love connection is oxytocin, a hormone that acts as a sort of bonding agent, making you feel warm and cuddly every time you come into physical contact and, like most sex chemicals, leaving you wanting more.

Stick around for a while and you'll eventually achieve a more

*L*OVE NOTE

CALL HIS FAVOURITE RADIO STATION WHEN YOU'RE SURE HE'LL BE LISTENING AND DEDICATE A SONG TO HIM.

permanent high. Endorphins are hormones released by the brain between three months and two years into the relationship, making people feel secure and loved.

Y IS FOR YACKETY-YACK

When it comes to sweet talk, the pitch of his voice is more important than what he actually says. A softer, lower tone can convey sexiness and vitality – even if you're just chatting about the weather. Which is why the phrase 'It's so hot' can sound sultry when breathed in a candyfloss whisper and like a weather report when uttered in the tone of Michael Fish.

Z IS FOR ZEST FOR LIFE

To discover what people look for in a mate, sociologist Dr Susan Sprecher conducted a cross-cultural survey of 1,667 men and women in the US, Japan and Russia. In all three countries, character ranked right up there with looks. So, you can suck in your stomach, fluff your hair and redo your lipstick, but you'll remain a sexual wallflower if no one's home personality-wise. Let's thank the love gods for that! ∎

Jumping
THE GUN

Assuming all has gone according to plan and he is gagging to marry you – joke, sorry – to ravish you, don't ever make the mistake of thinking 'No, no, I needn't shave my legs tonight because I will absolutely not sleep with him until the 15th date' or 'I am going to wear my grey period knickers because that will ensure I don't sleep with him tonight.'

ANNE FOUGEDOIRE

FROM THE MOMENT YOU DECIDE YOU WANT HIM, START PREPARING YOURSELF. THIS MEANS TOTAL DEFORESTATION.

The simple truth is that you may (as you realise he kisses like a god and merely feeling his arms around you makes you want to rip off his clothes and pin him to the floor) change your mind suddenly, then be faced with the bittersweet realisation that he is going to try to remove your grey period knickers with his teeth. In all honesty, by this stage, he wouldn't really care if you were wearing purple pantaloons.

However, being a great seductress is a state of mind as much as anything else, and if you feel uncomfortable your mood will communicate itself to him and kill the atmosphere stone dead. From the minute you decide you want him, start preparing yourself. This means total deforestation – underarms, legs, bikini line and, when you have a bikini line wax, don't be shy, demand as much off as you want – any stray hairs on

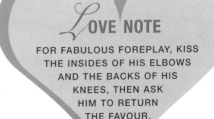

*L*OVE NOTE

FOR FABULOUS FOREPLAY, KISS
THE INSIDES OF HIS ELBOWS
AND THE BACKS OF HIS
KNEES, THEN ASK
HIM TO RETURN
THE FAVOUR.

LOVE NOTE

GIVE YOUR PARTNER A SENSUAL
HEAD AND FACE MASSAGE –
HE'LL BE PUTTY IN
YOUR HANDS!

your bottom – order her to whip them off. No one's pretending it's dignified but better your beautician thinks 'My, this woman's hairy'* than the dream man. (Although if he did, and worse, mentioned it, you would be justified in dumping him forthwith – shallow git.)

Other precautions: don't wear tights. Just don't. They have horrible gussets and are as sexy as a bin of maggots. Men hate them, and any enjoyment of getting it on with the man you lust after is ruined by you thinking 'He's going to see my heavy duty tights.'

Trouble is, the alternative is stockings – and although stockings are sexy, they also scream 'I've made the biggest effort in the world, I've trussed myself up like a chicken and worn these just for you'. At this, the game-playing stage, you don't want him to think this is the norm – unless you don't have a job you won't have time to

wear stockings every day. You want him to think of stockings as an occasional bonus. Seduction doesn't stop after you've got his boxers off. It should continue for as long as the relationship lasts. Some women avoid the tights/stockings dilemma by wearing trousers or going bare-legged – fine if you are dark-skinned or have a tan (or fake stuff that doesn't turn you orange) – not so fine if you have legs like Roquefort cheese.**

* Don't delude yourself you're any hairier than the rest of womankind – the majority of us are reasonably furry, it's normal.
** If it's a tights-or-nothing situation, wear the horrid things, but if he starts fumbling in the gusset area your best bet is to curl down and peel them off before he registers. You will, of course, have taken off your shoes first. Practise this manoeuvre in the privacy of your bathroom until you have it down to a slinky art.

REAL SEDUCTION, REAL NIGHTMARE
■ Elizabeth, 25: 'I was at college. It was the end of term ball. I knew exactly who I wanted to seduce and exactly what I was going to wear to do it. I invited this guy Gareth – I was friendly with the group of guys he lived with but it was quite a statement to have

invited him. He was lovely about it – he sent me a bouquet of red roses before the ball, the first flowers I'd ever received from a man. I had bought a long black clingy dress but the only problem was my stomach bulged. So I went to Marks & Spencer and bought really big granny pants to squash it in. Elasticised tummy panel, up to the waist, beige hue, the works. All went as planned, the snogging, the groping, and it was only when he slid his hand up my dress when I realised – the pants! He was such a sweet guy I'm sure he wouldn't have cared but I did. I couldn't stand him to know I was dressed in Victorian pants so I pushed his hands away. Actually, it worked out. He realised nothing was going to happen that night, and very sweetly kissed me goodbye at my door. We got it together a few days later. I was wearing my flimsiest, sexiest pants, if you must know.' ∎

HOW TO LOOK LIKE A LOVE GODDESS

Can someone please explain why a big spot always appears on your chin on the morning of your hot date? Here we answer your most commonly asked pre-date beauty questions.

My lipstick always gets on my, teeth and no one ever tells me. How can I keep my smile smudge–free?

First, find a friend who lets you know when you have stuff on your teeth. You should also follow make-up artist Maria Verel's lipstick-locking steps. Line and fill in lips with a lip pencil that matches your lipstick. Next, apply your lipstick over the liner but avoid the inner edges of your lips – that's the trouble zone. (To be on the safe side, put your finger in your mouth and pull it out.) Then blot your lips with a tissue and apply a colour sealer to set your lipstick until you wash it off.

'If your lips are chapped, however, you might find a sealer drying,' says Verel. If so, use a lip stain that blots on like ink and top it with a lip gloss for extra sexy shine.

My legs are so dry they flake and look dandruffy when I wear tights. What's can I do?

When you repeatedly wear stockings, the nylon fibres scrape against the dry skin cells on your legs and slough the cells off, resulting in all those flakes. The best way to slow the snow is to get rid of that layer of scaly skin regularly. At least once a week, soak in a bath and scrub your legs with a body-specific exfoliator to remove dead skin cells. Maintain a smooth surface with a daily dose of an AHA body cream, which both exfoliates and hydrates.

ANNE FOUGEDOIRE FERREZ

Why am I not supposed to squeeze blackheads, but it's OK for a beauty therapist to do it?

We do understand the satisfaction you can get from taking matters into your own hands by squeezing every little black dot (actually, it's just discoloured oil clogging pore opening). But in truth, that's no way to handle your face. Skin pros use a certain technique to extract gunk from pores with their fingers that would be virtually impossible for you to do yourself (mainly because of the angles and the difficulty of getting an up-close, well-lit look at your skin). So any pinching, pressing or squeezing you try at home can do more damage than good. You might push the oil deeper into the pore and cause a pimple, leave a small bruise, mini-crater or infection-prone cut on the skin's surface – all of which look much worse than a blackhead. But if your complexion's in need of a clean sweep, it's possible to banish blackheads without wielding your fingers.

First, massage a gentle exfoliator onto your face to loosen the clogs. Then pat your skin dry and apply a clay mask for five minutes to draw the blackheads out of your pores. Finally, rinse off with a cool wet flannel to reveal your new, spot-free complexion.

*L*OVE NOTE

HAVE WILD SEX, SNUGGLED UP TOGETHER IN BED, WHILE A THUNDERSTORM RAGES OUTSIDE.

I have a mole with a hair sticking out of it. First, how can I know it's not cancerous? Second, should I pluck it or snip it?

It might look ominous, but hair growing from a mole does not indicate skin cancer. Although cancerous skin discolourations can sprout strands, it's the appearance of the mole, not any hair growth, that you should pay attention to. Also, if the mole itself seems to be growing larger or changing shape, you should get it checked out by your doctor. Removing the hair from the mole won't put you at any greater risk from skin cancer. So go ahead: tweeze it, snip it, or zap it with electrolysis.

How can I tell the difference between the start of a bad breakout around my lips and herpes?

A spot and a cold sore can look identical in their early stages, so distinguishing between them is a matter of tuning in to what you feel rather than what you see. A few days before a cold sore appears, you may feel itching or tingling on your lip, but when a spot's on the way the area can be tender, rather than itchy. In the next stage, when the mysterious red bump does sprout, the pain factor is another indicator. When you touch a spot, it might hurt a little, but touching a cold sore will make you wince with pain. There is very little difference between the strain of herpes virus that appears on lips, but to be sure, ask your doctor. If you're certain it's a spot, dry it up fast with salicylic acid.

Is there any way to make pubic hair less wiry?

Salons don't yet offer relaxing and styling services for pubic hair, but you can soften the texture of your down-there hair with any regular conditioner designed to smooth curly hair. But the best way to make pubic hair seem softer is to trim it to a quarter-inch length so it lies flat.

On a recent date, I had noticeable BO. What emergency measure can I take in this oh–so–awkward stinky situation?

Whether it was nerves or a steamy session with your new man that made you break a sweat, any moisture on your body is a breeding ground for bacteria. The BO smell comes from the break-down of the by-products of all those bacteria. If possible, have a quick underarm wash using the antibacterial soap in the ladies' room. This will diminish your smell but won't ward off any new bacteria, so you may have to repeat mid-date.

Is it normal to have a few stray hairs around your nipples? And if so, is it OK to remove them?

Unfortunately, random nipple hairs are common for many women and, due to hormone fluctuations or extra-hairy genes, they're likely to return no matter what you do, so it's best to keep the process simple. Depilatories and wax work, but the aureola can be too sensitive for those methods. The cheapest and quickest method is tweezing, which only hurts for a second. Use slant-tipped tweezers to grab the hair as close to the skin as possible and always pull in the direction of the hair's growth.

What's the best at–home method to minimise lip hair?

If you're considering the bleaching route, ask yourself this: is a blonde moustache really any better than a dark one? No. So it's best to get rid of the hair completely. If you're nervous about waxing, try a cream depilatory – it's the easiest and most painless method for a smooth upper lip. Do a patch test first to make sure you're not allergic, then use the cream once a week.

How can I hide huge, red spots?

Large, subsurface spots are not classic pimples and under no circumstances should you squeeze them, however tempting it may seem. They're called cystic acne and are the result of an infection deep under the skin's surface. If you are constantly plagued by these underground eruptions, ask your GP to give your spot a shot of diluted cortisone that will shrink it in a day or two.

In the meantime, you can cover it, but not with regular concealer. If the skin is inflamed, ordinary make-up won't stick to it. As with any concealer, it's important to find the colour that matches your skin tone precisely, but if you can't find the perfect match, blend two together to create your own customised colour. To apply, dab the tiniest amount onto your spot, then pat with your fingers to blend.

All I need is the air that
I breathe
And to love you.

Hammond/Hazlewood,
as sung by The Hollies

TAMARA SCHLESINGER

What do you do when the man of your dreams just wants to be friends?

I'd pin him against a wall and make wanton love to him. I'd start by exploring his mouth, move slowly down to his neck and then just keep going in that general direction.

I rehearse this little seduction scene in my head whenever I can, perfecting the details (tongue or lips for that bit?), deciding the

Love
ME DO

atmosphere (background Eddi Reader or erotic silence?) and planning the location (my bedroom or his?). It's a great fantasy. And it would be all the more exciting if there were even the remotest chance of it ever being played out. But I know better. I know this

scene is destined to take place only in my head. Because I've succumbed to an age-old affliction – unrequited love.

And that's the reason why my fantasy fades. Because my common sense always flattens the romantic daydreams, and I see the

ERIC MCNATT

scene as it would really happen.
'What the hell are you doing?'
he'd yell. 'Gerroff! I thought we
were friends...'

We are. And that's the problem.
I don't want to be just friends. I
want him to be part of my life. But
he obviously doesn't feel the same

way. Sure, he likes me – we've
talked about it. He once looked
deep into my eyes and said,
'Whatever happens, I want us
always to be friends.'

Gee, thanks. It's got to stop.
This is how lives are wasted –
pining over never-to-bes, crying

for the moon. But, short of telling a good friend that I don't want to see him again, what can I do?

Marie did just that. 'Sean and I were friends for years. But after a while, whenever we got together, I knew I felt more for him than friendship. For a long time, I didn't say anything, I just tried to figure out if he might feel the same. But he only contacted me once every few weeks and was never jealous if I mentioned a new boyfriend – I could have choked him! Then one

THE PROBLEM OF BEING IN LOVE WITH SOMEONE WHO JUST ISN'T INTERESTED IN YOU IS THE CONTINUAL FRUSTRATION.

night I told him how I felt. He was great. He said he thought I was wonderful, too. Of course he loved me, too... but just not in that way. I spent a lot of time just wishing my life away. I got more depressed every time we met because I kept hoping that maybe... It took a year before I realised he was never going to feel the same for me and finally I thought, "Enough." I met him one last time and said goodbye. I still miss him.'

Walking away from unrequited love can't be compared with splitting up with someone you've had a long relationship with. At least then you've had a chance. The problem with being in love with someone who isn't interested in you as a partner is the continual frustration, the self-deception, the frantic re-organising of your entire life around vague notions of what he might do if you do this – or that. Worst of all is the continual hope. It makes you misinterpret everything he does. You convince yourself that his every kind gesture camouflages love, every kiss on the cheek becomes some smouldering passion held in check. Because it's unbearable to think that on the cheek is the only place he wants to kiss you.

Infatuation, lust, call it what you want – it isn't love. It will never be love. He just doesn't feel the same

ANNA PALMA

way as you do, so there will never be any relationship. Even if you go to bed with him, the closeness may deepen your feelings but it won't change his. He won't wake up next morning and suddenly be in love with you.

I found it difficult to accept that I could feel so strongly for someone but he could not feel the same way about me. Jung said, 'Don't ask why, ask what for?' So I stopped asking why he didn't feel as I did and began to look at what had attracted me to him in the first place. What did I need that he provided? He'd sneaked up on my affections like the tide. He was gentle, quiet and unassuming – an idealistic and a romantic – and this was what I missed in my life. Perhaps what I needed, then, wasn't so much him but a little more of me – the way I used to be.

Of course, love is always worth fighting for – if you both feel the same way. If only one of you feels strongly, by all means try, try, try again – but then forget it. There are too many other men out there who might love you, given a chance.

It's very easy to say I'm just going to walk away from it but, as I'm not making so much as a dent in his indifference, that's what I have to do. Even though I'll miss the high of being in love with him, the masochistic thrill of waiting for

I'M CERTAIN LOVE WILL COME ONE DAY – IT JUST WON'T HAVE HIS EYES, THAT'S ALL.

his phone call, the wondering if maybe this time... More importantly, I'll miss him. I'll always regret losing our friendship. After all, that kind of love is precious. Of course I want to keep him in my life. But I just don't have the stomach for such self-inflicted pain. Better to cut my losses now, I think, rather than stay in this limbo. Pain, grief, healing, whole. It comes in that order. You can't heal if you won't move away from the pain.

For me, love will have to wait. I'm certain it'll come one day – it just won't have his eyes, that's all. Right now, I'm going to move away from the pain. I'm going to arrange to meet him and tell him that I won't be seeing him again – not because I don't care for him, but because I do. Will he protest? Perhaps a little. But not enough. And that's how I'll know I've done the right thing. ∎

*L*OVE NOTE
THERE'S NOTHING LIKE THE SMELL OF FRESH SHEETS TO GET YOU IN THE MOOD. SPRINKLE A FEW DROPS OF ESSENTIAL OIL ON THEM.

Astro-sex
COMPATIBILITY CHART

FEMALE \ MALE	ARIES	TAURUS	GEMINI	CANCER	LEO
ARIES	Fiery pulse-raiser	Spicy sensuality	Conversation stopper	Sensual dream	Spontaneous, hot
TAURUS	Spicy sensuality	Magnetic affinity	Earthy sex boost	Close and warm	Passionate pulse-raiser
GEMINI	Conversation stopper	Earthy sex boost	Instant adrenalin peak	Steamy arousal	Super sexy
CANCER	Sensual dream	Close and warm	Steamy arousal	Sublimely orgasmic	Sensual but realistic
LEO	Spontaneous, hot	Passionate pulse-raiser	Super sexy	Sensual but realistic	Instant, fiery flower
VIRGO	Cool, potent buzz	Earthy affinity	Delicate sexual energy	Stormy differences	Sensual delight
LIBRA	Romantic lust	Hot and responsive	Luscious romance	Flowing and gentle	Vampy pulse-raiser
SCORPIO	Hypnotic energy flow	Sexy power struggle	Intensely different	Fabulous adrenalin rush	Steamy build-up
SAGITTARIUS	Instant arousal	Sexy differences	Magnificent sex rapport	Unpredictable responses	Super orgasmic peaks
CAPRICORN	Intense, erotic	Responsive and wild	Slow build-up	Challenging	Fiery response
AQUARIUS	Surprisingly potent	Unpredictable energy flow	Pacy and peaky	Cooling buzz	Amazing sexual link
PISCES	Sensually passionate	Dream-like responses	Demanding but sensual	Erotic arousal	Uneven energy

We've all been on the receiving end of that corny old chat-up line, 'What's your star sign?', but who knows, there may just be more than an element of truth in it. Check out our chart to discover just which star signs you're most compatible with and who offers you the most potential.

VIRGO	LIBRA	SCORPIO	SAGITTARIUS	CAPRICORN	AQUARIUS	PISCES
Cool, potent buzz	Romantic lust	Hypnotic energy flow	Instant arousal	Intense, erotic	Surprisingly potent	Sensually passionate
Earthy affinity	Hot and responsive	Sexy power struggle	Sexy differences	Responsive and wild	Unpredictable energy flow	Dream-like responses
Delicate, sexual energy	Luscious romance	Intensely different	Magnificent sex rapport	Slow build-up	Pacy and peaky	Demanding but sensual
Stormy differences	Flowing and gentle	Fabulous adrenalin rush	Unpredictable responses	Challenging	Cooling buzz	Erotic arousal
Sensual delight	Vampy pulse-raiser	Steamy build-up	Super orgasmic peaks	Fiery response	Amazing sex link	Uneven energy
Earthy, erotic	Sensual, romantic	Challenging	Hot responses	Luscious peaks	Sensually arousing	Perfect sex
Sensual, romantic	Blissful surges	Spontaneous thrill	Sublimely sensual	Erotic and demanding	Pacy and orgasmic	Sultry and intense
Challenging	Spontaneous thrill	Volatile libidos	Passionate but precarious	Intense energy flow	Wicked fling	Super sexy
Hot responses	Sublimely sensual	Passionate but precarious	Irresistible passion	Fiery and buzzing	Unpredictable and exciting	Sexy differences
Luscious peaks	Erotic and demanding	Intense energy flow	Fiery and buzzing	Earthy, erotic bliss	Luscious libido peaks	Sexy, uneven flow
Sensually arousing	Pacy and orgasmic	Wicked fling	Unpredictable and exciting	Luscious libido peaks	Delicious adrenalin build-up	Intense arousal
Perfect sex	Sultry and intense	Super sexy	Sexy differences	Sexy, uneven flow	Intense arousal	Blissfully orgasmic

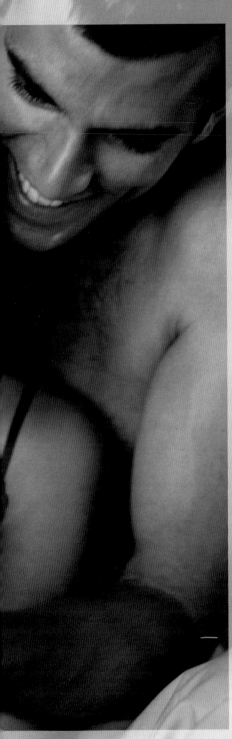

'The way to a man's heart is through his stomach.' Yes, we know it's an old cliché, but a spot of cunning cooking may help to make him yours.

PIECE OF
Cake

Show me someone who claims not to like chocolate desserts and I'll show you someone who's telling porky pies. Unfortunately, many orgasmically rich, gooey chocoholic dreams are a pain to make. But there is a way to wow your lover with a chocolate pud of distinction – just learn the secret of 'cheat's chocolate'. The key lies in a box of cake mix. Just mix, pour and bake, and save your creativity for the embellishing. Add a few extras and no one will know you don't deserve half the credit

Here are three cheat's chocolate delights. Each takes just minutes to prepare, they all taste better-than-great, and they'll fool him into thinking you're a chocolate champ. Which, of course, you are. With just a little help...

CATHERINE GRATWICKE

Cheat's chocolate soufflé cake

half a 500g (1lb 2oz) box of chocolate-cake mix, Betty Crocker if possible

Eggs (follow packet instructions for quantity)

Pinch of sugar

Butter, to grease ramekins

Icing sugar, to dust

SERVES: 8

1 Preheat the oven to 180°C/350°F/gas mark 4. Make the cake batter according to the instructions on the box, but with the following exception – separate the egg whites from the yolks instead of adding them whole to the mix. (Although you are using only half the packet, for this recipe you will need the number of eggs given in the instructions.) Put the egg yolks into the mix. Add a pinch of sugar to the egg whites and beat until they form soft peaks.

2 Grease 8 ramekins generously with butter. Dust the insides with a little icing sugar, shaking off the excess. When you're ready to cook, fold a spoonful of egg white into the cake mix, stir it in, then fold in the remainder quickly but evenly.

3 Divide the mixture between the ramekins, filling them to within 1.5cm (3/4in) of the top; don't be tempted to overfill. Bake in the centre of the oven, for around 20–30 minutes, until well risen. You can undercook these slightly if you like the centre a bit gooey. Remove from the oven, dust with icing sugar and serve immediately.

Cheat's chocolate baked Alaska

half a 500g (1lb 2oz) box of chocolate-cake mix

500ml (20fl oz) tub of chocolate ice-cream

2 egg whites

4 tbsp caster sugar

SERVES: 6

1 Make the cake according to the instructions on the box (remember that you are halving the quantities). Use a well-greased cake tin. When cooked, leave the cake to cool for about 15 minutes, then turn out onto a wire rack. After it has cooled to room temperature, cut into six and put the pieces on a large, non-stick baking sheet.

2 Cut the ice-cream block into six, putting a slice on each piece of cake.

LOVE NOTE

SPEND A WHOLE DAY BUILDING UP TO A NIGHT OF PASSION, FROM GENTLE CARESSING TO HUGGING TO MASSAGE.

Place in the freezer for 2 hours until the cake is well frozen.

3 Preheat the oven to 180°C/350°F/ gas mark 4. Beat the egg whites until they form soft peaks. Add the sugar gradually and beat to a medium-stiff meringue. Put a dollop of meringue on each cake and ice-cream portion. Bake near the top of the oven for 2–3 minutes, until the meringue is lightly browned. Eat at once.

Cheat's chocolate bite-sized bars

half a 500g (1lb 2oz) box of chocolate-cake mix

200g (7oz) packet of cream cheese

3–5 tbsp caster sugar

SERVES: 6–8

ERIC MCNATT

1 Make the cake according to the instructions on the box (remember that you are halving the quantities). Use a well-greased cake tin or roasting tin.

2 When it's cooked, leave the cake to cool for about 15 minutes, then turn it out onto a wire rack. After it has cooled to room temperature, cut it into small, bite-sized pieces.

3 Beat the cream cheese and sugar together until they are well blended. Leave to soften at room temperature, then spread evenly over the cake. Refrigerate the cake for at least

2 hours to give the cream cheese time to reset.

4 Serve the bars straight from the fridge or, for an even tastier version, place them under a blazing-hot grill for a couple of minutes. ■

Nobody dies from lack of sex. It's lack of love we die from.

Margaret Atwood

Recognising
WHAT'S NOT RIGHT
AND ENDING IT

Unfortunately, not all dates fizzle out
or softly roll over and die after some
minor communication glitch. Some
short relationships have to be prised
apart like a barnacle and the bottom
of a boat, or a limpet and whatever it
is a limpet sticks to.

ANNA PALMA

But if you're the one doing the dumping, there are a few simple pointers that can make the whole tricky task a little easier

The main tactic to minimise your feeling like a heel – and him feeling like a worthless piece of carpet fibre – is to keep the focus on you. And tell the truth (or a pretty close impersonation of it).

Say something like one of these tried-and-tested end lines:

● 'I realise this isn't working for me. I've had a lovely time with you/ you're a lovely man/I really care about you but I'm choosing not to take it any further.'

● 'The attraction I felt for you isn't developing into anything deeper.'

● 'I'm choosing not to do this anymore.'

These statements all fake responsibility for your choice, and takes it all off him being a terrible person or it being in any way his fault. He may argue, manipulate, whinge, lose his temper, storm out, cry, or instantly start flirting with someone else. Just be aware that's what he's doing and be aware you're sticking to your guns. Don't be tempted in a moment of weakness or misplaced responsibility to give him false hope that you may change your mind.

*L*OVE NOTE

A STOLEN KISS OR PINCH OF YOUR PARTNER'S BOTTOM DURING A BUSY DAY CAN PUT A TWINKLE IN YOUR EYE.

REMEMBER:

● You are not responsible for his feelings.

● You have the right to spend your time as you see fit.

● You have the right to say no and to end anything that isn't working for you.

But if all else fails, again, be a man. Just stop calling.

THE UNINTENTIONAL ART OF DUMPING

And then, of course, there's always the technique of dumping someone without actually meaning to, as one Cosmo reader found out to her cost:

■ There was a guy I went out with recently for a few dates, we had a nice time, he was sweet. One day we had a misunderstanding over the phone – with far-reaching consequences. He was on his mobile and I said 'I can't hear you, the line's breaking up'. He thought I said 'I can't bear you, we're breaking up'. After that he didn't call and I wasn't brave enough to enquire why. I only heard much later from a mutual friend that's what he thought had happened. One crackly phone call later and you're not going out anymore. **Marie, 26** ■

KATRINA WEBB

REAL-LIFE DATING
Dilemmas

If it was dreadful, console yourself with the fact your date may not have been as bad as these:

■ He was half an hour late and turned up with his best friend who insulted me – when I said I worked in a bank he replied, 'You look like you'd do something boring like that' – and bombarded me with questions as though he was a chaperone sussing me out for his friend. I felt furious, and wished to God I'd had my best friend there to even the odds. Believe it or not, mug that I am, I dated him twice after that and I realised he wasn't interested in a relationship at all really. Which was kind of symbolised by his bringing his mate along on a first date.
Katie, 24

ANNA PALMA

We were getting on really well and he said 'I find you really easy to talk to', which made me feel good. Then he told me he was in love with his ex and knew he would never feel that way about another woman. My face must have dropped and he said, 'Sorry, I needed to talk to someone about it and you're so understanding.'
Julie, 23

We were having a drink and a whole lot of people came over who he recognised but he didn't introduce me. I thought that was a bit rude. I said so, and he said 'I'm really sorry, I forgot your name'. It wasn't a good sign.
Debbie, 20

Last year, I went skiing with four friends. While we were standing in line for the chairlift, we realised one of us would have to sit with a stranger. I spotted a Ben Affleck lookalike waiting behind us and immediately volunteered to 'go it alone'. When it was my turn to ski up to the chairlift, I picked up a little too much momentum, so I reached out to my sexy partner's arm trying to slow myself down. Unfortunately, I succeeded in knocking him into the snow just as the lift scooped me up and carried me up the mountain alone!
Yvonne, 27

WHEN HE SAID 'I'M SORRY, I FORGOT YOUR NAME', IT WASN'T A SIGN THE DATE WAS GOING WELL.

I was so nervous with this guy, because I really liked him. But when we went out, I discovered he was a bit of a drinker, while I'm not. However, I stupidly felt I had to keep up with him. I was doing OK, then suddenly felt really drunk when we got outside the restaurant. Then – horror of horrors – I threw up all over him in the taxi. Needless to say, he didn't call me again. And I was too embarrassed to call him.
Caroline, 26

It was all going swimmingly, then he told me I was of the wrong religion and he'd sworn to himself he'd never date a non-Jewish woman. Which rather begged the question: why did you ask me out? I felt completely deflated, and the conversation just died after that.
Joanne, 27

One morning I locked eyes with a devastatingly handsome man in the stairwell of my office building – he was on his way up as I was heading down. I'd been trying to grab his attention for weeks so I tried to act sophisticated and gave him my best lustful stare. Not wanting to break the gaze as I turned the corner, I misplaced my foot and toppled down a whole flight of stairs. I lay there feeling sore and stupid, as he dashed down to help me up. He was so

gallant that, in between feeling a complete fool, I was totally smitten. We've been together for over a year now.
Sharon, 29

■ My then ex-boyfriend and I had been apart about eight months when he started dating another woman. One day, I ran into him at a bar and noticed he'd left his coat on a rack near the door. As I was leaving, I took out my perfume and sprayed it all over the collar of his jacket. I suppose his new girlfriend smelled it on him and they had a row. She dumped him and we were reunited. We've now been happily married for four-and-a-half years. He still doesn't know what brought us together again!
Rachel, 32

■ He spent the entire time constantly looking over his shoulder at other women. Then he had the cheek to ask me what I thought of one of them – a particularly stunning blonde. I just said 'We obviously have nothing in common', stood up and walked out.
Emma, 27

■ One night, my new boyfriend and I went to a fancy dress party. He dressed up as the Phantom

of the Opera and I went as a devil. During the party, I saw him making his way to the bedroom, where all our coats had been dumped. I quickly followed him inside and locked the door. I pounced on him before he could speak and started kissing him furiously. As I broke away, he let out a gasp and asked what I thought I was doing? To my utter horror, I had captured the wrong Phantom!
Wendy, 29

■ I was leaving my friend's office one afternoon when I overheard a conversation the receptionist was having with a really good-looking man. Apparently, he was trying to find out how to apply for a job with her company. As he walked out, I stopped him and introduced myself as the personnel director. I asked him if he'd like to discuss his qualifications over a drink. He agreed and drinks turned into dinner. Obviously, I couldn't help him get a job, but I had a great evening.
Beth, 27

■ I went on my first date with a gorgeous man the same day I had my tongue pierced. We went to the cinema and, in the middle of the film, he started kissing my neck

Love NOTE
BAT YOUR EYELASHES AGAINST HIS CHEEKS, LIPS, THE BOTTOMS OF HIS FEET OR ANYWHERE ELSE YOU FANCY.

and we became very passionate.
I totally forgot about the pain my
tongue was causing me, but then
my date started gagging. The
tongue stud had come loose and
was slipping down his throat! I'm
just glad it was dark so he couldn't
see how red my face was.
Helen, 28

■ I once messed up a blossoming
relationship because I acted like
I felt I should, rather than how I
wanted to. We were just getting to
know each other. We'd been out
once, he'd given me a chaste kiss
goodbye, then I'd been over to
his place where he'd cooked me
dinner and we'd talked and kissed
a little more. Then I invited him
over to me for dinner the following
Friday. If I'd been him, I would have
called the day before to confirm the
date was still on. But he didn't call
until two hours before he was
actually due at my house. By then,
I'd convinced myself he wasn't
going to turn up. So when he said
'Is it still on?', I pretended in a
mad attempt to be cool that I'd
forgotten and was now busy. His
voice went cold, and when I said
'But can we do it another time?',
he said 'Sure' and rang off. I did
phone him again but he was
always busy. It was my own fault
for trying to be too clever.
Jayne, 28

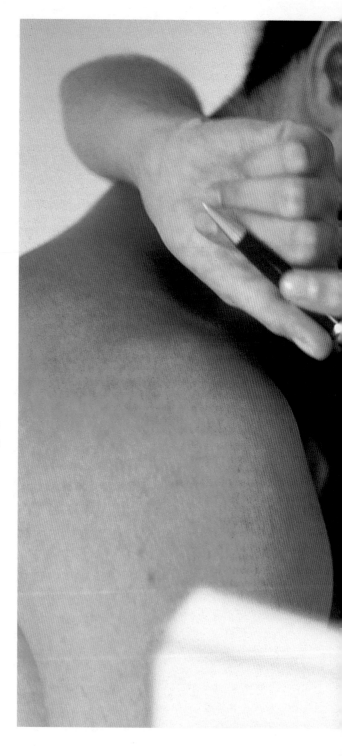

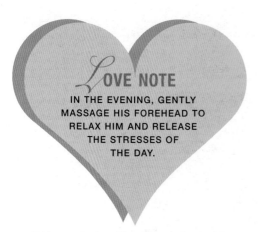

LOVE NOTE

IN THE EVENING, GENTLY
MASSAGE HIS FOREHEAD TO
RELAX HIM AND RELEASE
THE STRESSES OF
THE DAY.

■ I was just getting it together with this gorgeous guy. A friend was having a drinks party and I invited Pete. He had a dinner to attend but said he'd turn up later. I don't drink much at all, but that night I was so nervous I started knocking back neat tequila. By the time Pete arrived I was semi-comatose. All I really remember is Pete giving me a fireman's lift up to his room – it was the first time his flatmates had met me so it wasn't the greatest first impression. I think I must have hurled at some point because I woke up the next morning in Pete's bed feeling fine. He was sitting fully clothed in the middle of the room. He'd watched me all night to make sure I didn't expire. It wasn't my ideal seduction plan, but to his credit, I think he was only mildly horrified. Possibly he thought he'd seen me at my worst, so it could only get better! And it did...
Carla, 27

HE SAID 'YOU'RE THE WOMAN OF MY DREAMS, I THINK YOU'RE AMAZING AND WE COULD LIVE HAPPILY EVER AFTER'. THIS WAS WITHIN TWO HOURS.

AND THE WINNER IS...

■ We went for a coffee and to begin with he was OK. Then he said let's go to the park. It was a sunny day and we were just walking along when he produced his Walkman, and got me to listen to music he's made with his mates. Then he seemed to crumble up into a state of high anxiety and rushed off to the nearby shop, leaving me listening to mad loud rock music. He came back with loads of beer and at the same time is telling me he's a recovering alcoholic and just out of rehab for crack cocaine addiction. This isn't going too well, I thought. I'd better have a beer myself.

He had one beer and it was like someone had clicked a switch and he morphed into this complete nutter. He said, 'You're the woman of my dreams. I think you're amazing and we could live happily ever after'. This is within two hours. Then he launched into a story about how he had this incredible penis. 'I can take a woman to another dimension.'

He got more and more drunk and I said, 'This has been fun, but I'm going to go now.'

He grabbed my hand and said 'You're not going anywhere'. I was really scared he'd chase me down the street or something. I'd had a drink too and I wasn't really thinking straight. I suggested we went to a pub so I could dodge out more easily.

Then he took a call on his mobile and it sounded to me like he was making a drugs deal. He was muttering, 'a hundred, a hundred, meet me in Leicester Square'. I stood up in the pub and said I wasn't having this. He said 'I wasn't buying drugs, I was buying you jewellery because I love you so much.'

So I gathered my stuff together, and said 'This date is over.' He followed me all the way to the station, shouting at me all along the road. When I got home there were nine answerphone messages from him. I had to change my number to stop him calling **Gemma, 27** ■

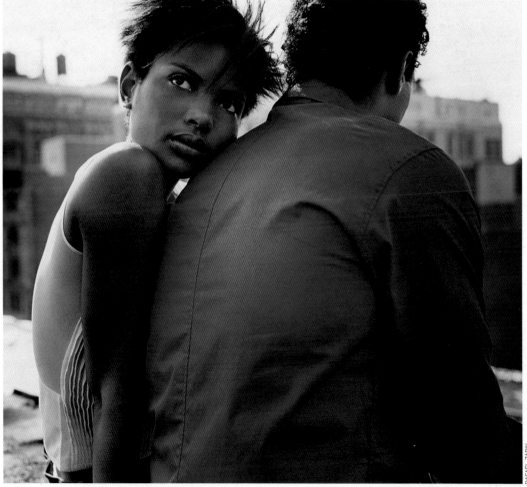

RAFAEL ZABIK

HOW TO

Keep Him

ERIC MCNATT

DO YOU
SABOTAGE YOUR RELATIONSHIPS WITHOUT REALISING IT ?

Do you rub out romances with your bitching and bullying, or suffocate them to death with your non-stop neediness? Take this quiz and learn how to squash the 'killer' instincts that leave your relationships DOA. You might even discover you already have the stuff to keep love alive.

1 When your current boyfriend asks about your exes, you answer that:

a You thought you'd found the right guy a few times, but each one broke your heart.
b Things didn't work out romantically, but you always ended up good friends.
c If there's justice, they'll face endless tax audits, parking tickets and root canal treatment.

2 Your man gets fired by his nightmare of a boss. Automatically, you:

a Insist that he moves right in with you; he needs all the cuddling he can get.
b Tell him he'd better land a job before your big romantic getaway – you're certainly not picking up the hotel bill.
c Take him to dinner, let him know you're there and help him write his CV.

3 You're in bed with him, but the way he's touching you reminds you of your gynaecologist – and not in a good sense. Your immediate move:

a Lie still. Only a total bitch would bust him on his sexual technique.
b Gently move his hand to a hotter spot.
c Tell him you're way too stressed-out for sex, then switch on the television.

4 You are on your way to a restaurant – the one he always gets lost trying to find. What do you say?

a 'I always get confused around here. It's a left turn up ahead, right?'
b 'Can we try to remember to take the left turn this time?'
c Nothing until it's too late. Naturally, you then take all the blame.

Love is always in the mood of believing in miracles.

John Cowper Powys

5 On your birthday your beau, who is on a tight budget, presents you with a home–cooked dinner and a sappy love song he wrote for you. Your reaction?

a 'Honey, I wouldn't trade you in for Donald Trump in a million years.'
b 'You shouldn't have gone to all that trouble. I could have cooked.'
c 'So, did you get me anything?'

6 After a toe–curling session of sex, you're up for pillow talk, but he's out for the count. You:

a Closely snuggle up to him – even after he tries to squirm over to the other side of the bed.
b Elbow him awake and inform him that post-coital cuddling is your absolute god-given right.
c Tell him gently the next morning that you'd like a little loving over the coming weekend, when his libido won't be the only thing that's 'up'.

7 After moving in together, you discover both of you now own twice as much stuff as you actually need. What to do?

a Make a deal. You'll ditch a chair if he'll sacrifice his plastic dishes.
b Insist he donates all his furniture to the local charity shop. After all, your belongings are far, far better.
c Offer to dump all your stuff. You know he'll pay you back – somehow.

8 On the night of your dinner party, he tells you his dad is scheduled for emergency gall–bladder surgery the next morning. How do you deal with it?

a Tell him the surgery is not until tomorrow; if he can't make it, he's history.
b Suggest he stops by for dessert – if he's not feeling too stressed.
c Immediately cancel the dinner. Your friends will understand; he very well might not.

9 For the third night this week, you're working late on a big proposal. Your man's complaining because he craves more time with you. You say:

a 'I'm sorry but I have to get this done. Let's make a proper date for the coming weekend.'

b 'How dare you whine at me – I thought I could at least count on you for a little support.'

c 'You're completely right. My boss hasn't bought my life. I'll be home in half an hour.'

10 He has an extremely annoying habit of picking at his teeth after dinner. What do you do?

a Joke that toothbrushes work even better than fingernails.

b Ignore it. So he's got a few bad habits.

c Point out his 'picking' problem while you're at dinner with friends – the sheer embarrassment ought to cure him pretty quickly.

SCORING

1	a-1	b-2	c-3
2	a-1	b-3	c-2
3	a-1	b-2	c-3
4	a-2	b-3	c-1
5	a-2	b-1	c-3
6	a-1	b-3	c-2
7	a-2	b-3	c-1
8	a-3	b-2	c-1
9	a-2	b-3	c-1
10	a-2	b-1	c-3

25 POINTS OR MORE:
Love Crusher

You're the Lee Harvey Oswald of love, rubbing out any potential for romance. Your 'passion assassin' tendencies may stem from having been let down previously – either during childhood or in an earlier relationship going really wrong. You feel that if you don't connive, bully and manipulate, your needs will never be met, says Susan Jeffers, author of *Opening Our Hearts to Men* (Fawcett). Or perhaps you're simply scared of intimacy, snuffing out a relationship before it has a chance to take hold.

So, how to stop the killer within? For starters, catch yourself every time you express feeling in terms of a put-down or anger, says Carolyn Bushong, author of *The Seven Dumbest Relationship Mistakes Smart People Make* (Villard). 'Try saying "I'm disappointed" or "I'm hurt" instead of "You insensitive pig". Even "I'm insulted" will do.'

Next, give yourself a quota of saying ten thank-yous to him a day – 'even if it's just because he brought you your morning coffee,' says Jeffers. Meanwhile, quit your bitching: 'If he feels appreciated, he'll be that much more loving.'

18 TO 24 POINTS:
Genius of Love

Of course, nobody's perfect, but when it comes to building a loving relationship, you're pretty darn close. Your secret is deceptively simple: a healthy sense of self-respect. Gently but firmly you show your man that you'll treat him with tenderness and consideration – as long as he returns the favour. 'This type knows how to call a guy on his bad behaviour without destroying him,' says Jeffers.

Also, you're not a needy person. 'You have a purpose in life beyond the relationship,' continues Jeffers. 'Your friends, your job, your participation in the community are important to you too. If the relationship ended tomorrow, you would hurt, but you know you would survive.' Ultimately, it's this love-him-but-can-live-without-him outlook that makes men so hot to be with you.

17 POINTS OR FEWER:
Love Fool

You must have the word 'doormat' tattooed on your forehead, given the way you allow men to walk all over you. The sad thing is, even when he does leave footprints all over your face, you cling even harder – which only serves to drive him further away. Says Jeffers: 'Healthy men are terrified of extreme neediness. They know they can't fill the void.'

Okay, so how to stop being the girl most likely to get ditched? First, pin-point those times you feel like you're bending too far backwards for a man. 'Ask

ADAM OLSZEWSKI

make your own demands, adds Dr Tanenbaum: 'If he suggests seeing a guy movie and you're in the mood for a chick flick, say "I was really looking forward to seeing *Bridget Jones's Diary* – do you mind?"' From there, it's far easier to work up to bigger demands and more important issues.

Lastly and most importantly, don't forget to get a life. After all, only when the relationship stops completely defining your entire life will you really find the guts to ask for what you want. You'll also stop being the queen of cling. 'By developing yourself,' explains Jeffers, 'you stop being so needy. You become a woman of substance – a woman whom a quality man can really appreciate and love.'

Love doesn't make the world go round.
Love is what makes the ride worthwhile.

Franklin P Jones

yourself, "Is this something I want to do – or am I doing it so he'll feel indebted to me?"' says Judith H Tanenbaum, a Manhattan psychiatrist. You can also

EX-*wreckers* CONFESS

Learn from the love mistakes these Cosmo women made.

■ 'I used to be a merciless teaser. I knew I'd gone too far when a guy I really liked stormed out on me one night. So I had two choices: either lose my mean streak or lose my man.'

■ 'When it came to fights, I'd bring up some "crime" a guy had committed two months before. Then I learned to stick to the matter at hand. Now the arguments hardly ever escalate.'

■ 'Needy was my middle name. I'd call and pester a guy until he started to let his voicemail pick up. Now when I'm about to say "I need…", I stop myself and think, does this really matter?'

■ 'I live with a man but was always coming on to other guys – I just didn't want to miss out on the possibility of something better. Then one day it struck me: I was as bad as all those commitment-phobic men.'

■ 'I was the mistress of the perfect put-down, until the awful time he asked me whether I thought he'd gained weight. When I answered that I now knew the difference between dating a babe and 'Babe', he looked so hurt that I started crying.'

■ 'I was the princess of pouting. If he worked late on a Friday night, I'd sulk for the rest of the weekend. He finally figured out how to get back at me: simply ignore me. That took the pout off my pucker.'

10 SIGNS THE RELATIONSHIP IS OVER

1 Over dinner he excuses himself to go to the loo and never comes back.

2 You finally figure out why his flatmate doesn't like him bringing anyone back – she's his wife.

3 When you call him, the only person you reach is the operator telling you the number has become an ex-directory one.

4 You read his engagement announcement in the paper… and you're not the bride.

5 You're served with a restraining order.

6 You see him on *Jerry Springer*, revealing his secret crush… on your brother.

7 You resort to sending yourself flowers on major occasions, so your friends won't realise he 'doesn't believe in material gifts'.

8 He emails you a note, asking you to post him his toothbrush.

9 You spot him on *Crimewatch*.

10 After moving in, you realise he doesn't just love his dog, he *loves* his dog.

THE COSMO
Man Test

SEVEN SNEAKY WAYS TO FIND OUT IF HE'S THE ONE (WITHOUT ACTUALLY ASKING)

Everything's looking good – he laughs at your jokes, makes you sizzle in the bedroom and even remembered your birthday. But before you book the church and buy the dress, remember: this is a man you're dealing with and men are notorious for saying one thing while thinking another.

ANNA PALMA

Whether you've been together for five minutes or five years, he would rather be condemned to a football season without beer than be hit with a 'where do we stand' quiz. So, if you want to suss out how your relationship rates, get sneaky with our seven cunning read-your-man set-ups. Each one reveals how he feels in less than 10 seconds and all you need is a watch, a camera, a pen and a sweet in its wrapper. Of course, you don't want to ditch a love-worthy male for nothing – so take into account his mood, the setting and your (almost) impeccable female intuition as you put him through the following revealing tests...

WATCH HIM CAREFULLY

The truth test: **While you are both talking at a table, absent-mindedly slide your watch off your wrist and into his personal space (within 18 inches of him) while you casually continue the conversation. What does he do with the watch?**

a Picks it up and keeps it close to the table.
b Grips it between his thumb and finger, then hands it back.
c Rubs it, traces it with his fingers or twirls it in his hand.
d Pushes it back to you, barely touching it or does nothing with it.
e Covers it with his hand (or even puts it on).

Desire decoded: 'The way he handles intimate items that belong to you represents how he'd like to handle you,' explains body language expert Jan L Hargrave, author of *Freeway of Love* (Kendall/Hunt). Holding onto the watch (a), fondling it (c), or drawing it closer to him (e), mimics what he's thinking of doing to you (if he runs it across his lips, slowly, you're in for a sizzling evening!). If he barely touches your timepiece (b) or pushes it back towards you (d), he's not very relationship-ready right now.

THE WRITE STUFF

The truth test: **Make up some excuse to get your man to write down both of your names. How does your name look compared to his?**

a Both names are about the same size and the writing looks similar.
b Your name is more slanted or is noticeably smaller than his.
c Your name is written in angular script.
d His is legible, while yours is illegible.
e Yours is bigger and blockier than his.

Desire decoded: Hand-writing experts believe the way he writes your name compared to his own tells you where you stand. If he writes your name in bigger, blockier letters than his (e), he worships the ground you walk on. Angular letters (c) reveal revved-up sexual feelings for you. If the writing looks about the same with both names (a), you have a balanced relationship which may need more passion. If your name is smaller or more slanted than his (b), he's not seriously committed right now. If he scribbles your name illegibly (d), he doesn't see the two of you as a couple at all.

POSING A PROBLEM?

The truth test: **In a bar or at party, tell your man to wait while you go the ladies, then observe his pose once he spots you coming back. How does he hold himself when he notices you returning?**

a He leans forward, his feet pointing towards you.
b He leans away from you.
c His legs are spread, his thumbs hooked in his pockets or belts loops.
d His arms are crossed over his chest and he looks away from you.

e He stretches out an arm to touch or greet you.

Desire decoded: The way a man stands in front of you reveals how open he feels towards you. Leaning in feet first (a) means he's interested, and if he reaches into your personal space to touch you (e), bingo! He is seriously into you. Touching his jeans or his belt loops (c) says there's sex on the horizon – subliminally, he is directing your attention down there. If he leans back (b) he may need more space. Crossed arms (d) indicate he's blocking out the chance for long-term romance.

THE COLOUR OF LOVE

The truth test: **Has he been drawn to a particular colour recently? Ask him a question which brings up the subject, such as, 'If you were to buy a new shirt, what colour would you choose?' What's on his colour conscience?**

a Green.
b Black.

c Red.
d Grey.
e Blue.

Desire decoded: 'The colour he's attracted to at the moment illustrates whether he's ready for a serious relationship right now,' says Suzy Chiazzari, author of *The Complete Book Of Colour* (Element). Red (c) is a high-energy, passionate colour – if that's the shade he chose, look out, he has pure lust on his mind. Blue (e) reveals a calmer, more romantic vibe; green (a) means he's not feeling particularly passionate towards you – but he could be swayed. Black (b) shows he's too focused on his own needs and won't be able to give you the attention you deserve, while grey (d) demonstrates he's keeping a part of himself hidden – so you'll need to work hard at to uncover it.

EXPOSE THE TRUTH

The truth test: **Ask a friend to take a photo of the just two of you standing side by side, or look at your body**

language in your latest holiday snaps. What part of you is his hand touching in the photo?

a The shoulder furthest from him.
b Your upper back.
c Your neck or hair.
d The shoulder closest to him.
e The small of your back or around your waist.

Desire decoded: 'The way he stands next to you in a photo demonstrates what he wants other people to know about you as a couple,' explains Hargrave. A man who limits his touch to the part of your body closest to his (d) is trying to keep space between you. If he puts his hand on your neck or hair (c), he feels possessive, physically and sexually. If his hand is around your shoulder (a) he's indicating your relationship might work best on a platonic level. If he touches your lower back or puts his arm around your waist (e) he feels emotionally intimate towards you. If he touches your upper back (b) he's showing affection, but may need some encouragement to feel sexually intimate.

ANNA PALMA

LOOK INTO HIS SOLE

The truth test:

Compliment his shoes – give them a long glance and watch how he reacts. What does he do with his feet?

a Keeps them planted right where they are and says 'Thanks!'
b Nervously slides them under his chair trying to hide them.
c Holds his feet out so you can take a better look.
d Crosses his legs, trying to cover one shoe with the other.
e Smiles, bends down and pulls at his socks.

Desire decoded: Surprise! If your man tugs at his socks (e), he's sending you sweet flirtatious signals, says Hargrave. 'It's an unconscious move people make when they are especially attracted to someone,' she says. If he wants to get his feet closer to you (c), he's confident of his attraction to you. If he tucks them under his chair (b), he's not ready for true intimacy. If his feet stay planted on the floor (a),

he's so laid back he's virtually horizontal and doesn't care about you either way. But if he crosses one foot over his knee or tries to cover a shoe with his hand (d), he's trying to hide from you and has something he's not ready to share.

CHOCOLATE CHECK-UP

The truth test: While sitting down talking, offer him a sweet in an individual wrapper. After he eats the sweet, what does he do with the wrapper?

a Rolls it into a ball.
b Twists it up into one long strip.
c Tears it into tiny strips.
d Sculpts it into a silly shape.
e Scrunches it up then flattens it out over and over again.

Desire decoded: 'It may a little sound bizarre, but channelling nervous energy into a sweet wrapper reveals a lot about what we're feeling inside,' says Murray Langham, counsellor and author

of *Chocolate Therapy* (Souvenir). A man whose veins are coursing with sexual energy will tear the paper up (c), whereas if he keeps scrunching and smoothing it out (e) he's trying to make everything perfect with you. Rolling a wrapper into a little ball (a) means he likes you in a no-stress, friendly way which means your relationship may have lasting potential once you feel comfortable together. Twisting (b) shows he's uncertain about how things stand, while making little foil animals (d) means he's distracted – he may be more interested in sculpting a paper dog than in you!

Now check your answers against the Romance Scorecard overleaf.

*L*OVE NOTE
BOOK A SURPRISE WEEKEND TRIP TO PARIS AND KISS IN THE MOONLIGHT OUTSIDE THE SACRE COEUR.

ROMANCE SCORECARD

How many times did he react with an A, B, C, D or E? Read on for an instant summing up of his body language in terms of your future together.

MOSTLY As
Friends for now

Your man is a solid, sensible lover who's more interested in getting to know you than jumping straight into bed or racing down the aisle. He's not about to rush headlong into romance so just focus on having fun. Proving you're into him as a person – not just a sex object – will wipe out his worry about whether this is the real thing. Pressure him to profess his love and he'll back off – for good.

MOSTLY Bs
He's hesitant, honey

Don't hold your breath. This man is going to take his time to decide whether you're the love of his life – or a woman he's just terribly fond of. He wants his life to be settled before he takes on a serious love affair.

Expressing an interest in his work and goals will show you like him for who he is. Give him the time he needs and he'll come round – eventually.

MOSTLY Cs
Lusty lad!

If you're looking for a good time in the bedroom, you've hit nookie nirvana with this one – but he's likely bail out as soon as you say the words 'joint mortgage'. Build intimacy gradually with friendly, joint activities, such as cooking a pre-passion dinner together, rather than just hitting the sheets. Before you know it, he'll be head over heels (and not only when in a Kama Sutra position).

MOSTLY Ds
No way, José

Ouch! This man's not for biting the bait. Timing is everything – and you both know deep down that a relationship is the last thing he wants in his life right now. Do him a favour by backing off – give him the breathing space he's gasping for or you'll

suffocate all hope. Hold back for a while and he'll be more open to the idea of taking things to a higher level.

MOSTLY Es
Ready romantic

Are you looking for love? Let's hope so because this man is supremely smitten – he pines for you as a friend and a lover. The only thing you could do to dissuade him now? Sleep with his best friend (although, even then, he might still forgive you). Here is a man who will love you until *Scream* runs out of sequels. This is it. Roll out the big white dress and introduce him to your parents (or is that the other way round?). Congratulations. He's in lurrvvve! ■

*L*OVE NOTE
TRY RUNNING YOUR TONGUE SUGGESTIVELY ALONG THE NAPE OF HIS NECK WHILE HE BRUSHES HIS TEETH.

Celebrate a lazy, love-in weekend with a sexy scrumptious feast between the sheets. Breakfast in bed has never tasted so good.

Sunday Girl

MENU

TO DRINK
Rich hot chocolate with pink foam

TO EAT
Tropical granola crunch with yogurt and honey

Brioche cinnamon toast with vanilla seeds

American pancakes with raspberry and maple sauce

JAMES MITCHELL

HOT CHOCOLATE WITH PINK FOAM

For a devilishly naughty start to the weekend try this sweet treat.

PREPARATION AND COOKING TIME: 10 MINUTES

SERVES: 2

50g/2oz plain chocolate (with at least 70% cocoa solids), broken into pieces
1 pint milk
8 pink marshmallows
Nutmeg

Divide the chocolate between two mugs. Heat the milk in a pan until almost simmering, then pour just enough into each mug to cover the chocolate. Put the remaining milk back on a very low heat, add the marshmallows and whisk until they are melted. Top up the mug with the pink foam and serve with a sprinkling of nutmeg and a spoon to make the most of the chocolate!

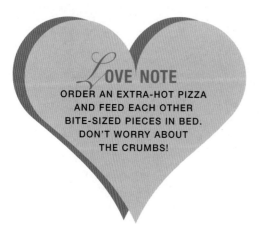

LOVE NOTE
ORDER AN EXTRA-HOT PIZZA AND FEED EACH OTHER BITE-SIZED PIECES IN BED. DON'T WORRY ABOUT THE CRUMBS!

TROPICAL GRANOLA CRUNCH

These crispy honeyed oats taste divine when they're still warm.

PREPARATION TIME: 10 MINUTES

COOKING TIME: 20 MINUTES

SERVES: 8

680g/11/2lb rolled oats
100g/4oz desiccated coconut
150g/6oz honey
100g/4oz light brown sugar
75g/3oz butter
170g/7oz tropical dried fruit
Small tub yogurt
Honey to serve

Put the oats into a bowl and stir in the coconut. Melt the honey, sugar and butter in a pan and bring to the boil. Keep stirring until the sugar dissolves, then pour over the oats and mix well. Spread the mixture on a baking sheet and toast in a low oven for 20 minutes, stirring every 10 minutes until golden. Set aside to cool. Add the fruit and serve with yogurt and honey. Store the rest in an airtight container.

BRIOCHE CINNAMON TOAST

Toast the weekend with this sweetly spiced bread – it's delicious served with fresh fruit.

PREPARATION TIME: 6 MINUTES

COOKING TIME: 1 MINUTE

SERVES: 2

Seeds from one vanilla pod

100g/4oz granulated sugar

2 tsp cinnamon

150g/6oz softened butter

1 loaf brioche

Put the vanilla seeds into a bowl with the sugar and cinnamon and mix together with a wooden spoon. Add the butter and blend until smooth. (Alternatively, you can mix these four ingredients with an electric hand mixer.) Thickly slice and toast your brioche and spread some cinnamon butter on each slice. Serve while hot on its own, or with grilled peaches or fresh raspberries on top.

AMERICAN PANCAKES

These yummy miniature pancakes are the perfect size for feeding to each other.

PREPARATION TIME: 12 MINUTES
COOKING TIME: 10 MINUTES
SERVES: 2

For the pancakes:

150g/4fl oz milk

1 egg, beaten

25g/1oz butter, melted

175g/7oz plain flour

1/2 tsp salt

2 tbsp caster sugar

1 tbsp baking powder

2 heaped tbsp cottage cheese

Extra butter for the pan

For the sauce:

80ml/3 fl oz maple syrup

25g/1oz butter

100g/4oz raspberries

Stir together the milk, egg and melted butter. Sift the dry ingredients into a separate bowl, combine with the egg mix, followed by the cottage cheese (don't worry if the mixture isn't smooth). Heat a little butter in a frying pan over a medium heat, then ladle in the batter to make rounds the size of small saucers. Cook until bubbles form on the top, then flip them over and cook until golden. Warm the syrup and butter together in a saucepan, add the raspberries, pour over the pancakes to serve.

PETER BUCKINGHAM

FOOD OF LOVE

Here's how to tell if he's hungry for love by how he nibbles his lunch.

Long luncher: If he savours every morsel, he's one for sensual, teasing sex. He'll take it slowly with lots of foreplay, but this may mean he suffers from delayed ejaculation. **Drive him wild:** With sensual massage and sensuous oral sex.

Wild wolfer: A man who clears his plate in minutes has a huge sexual appetite. He's eager to bed you, but foreplay may be an alien concept, and his frenzy might signal premature ejaculation. **Drive him wild:** Take him by surprise – any time, any place, anywhere.

Plate picker: Playing with food and a small appetite can mean he's a dreamer – more goes on in his head than in his bed. He's a sucker for mental seduction, be sensitive to his moods and share fantasies. **Drive him wild:** Erotica pushes him over the edge.

Secret scoffer: If he prefers to eat in private, he's shy but willing. Take it slow – you'll have to take the initiative but the rewards will be well worth it. **Drive him wild:** Show your pleasure with the Kama Sutra. ■

6 LOVE MYTHS
— busted!

Want to get closer to your man? Stop clinging to the old commitment clichés and learn the modern rules of romantic bliss. We spill the success secrets of couples who stay in love and in lust.

JUST BECAUSE LUST LEVELS SHIFT OVER TIME DOESN'T MEAN THE HOTTEST PART OF YOUR RELATIONSHIP WILL BE A CUP OF COCOA.

When Cupid strikes, you know just what to expect, right? Total joy and happily-ever-afterhood. After all, you've seen it played out a million times in every Meg Ryan film you've ever watched. Well, sit down, we have some news to break. The truth is, those sweet stories are totally out of touch with what it truly takes to make a successful relationship. 'We're brought up with the concept of fairy-tale love, but those overly syrupy and simplified stories have it all wrong,' says Josey Vogels, author of *Dating: A Survival Guide From The Frontlines* (Adams Media). 'If you believe them, and base your expectations on them, you could set your love-affair on the fast track to failure.' Here, we unmask six toxic love myths, then offer Cosmo's own lasting-love code.

LOVE MYTH *1*

Happy couples are always madly, deeply in lust.

Reality check: Even those embarrassingly passionate couples have days when sex doesn't come first. 'Relationships go through cycles,' explains Lillian Glass, author of *The Complete Idiot's Guide To Understanding Men And Women* (Alpha Books). 'Sometimes sex is a priority and sometimes – as relationships develop, stresses come and go, and hormones change – other activities rank top of the list. The evenings you curl up together and watch TV all night are a much bigger piece of the passionate pie than you think.' Cosmo's mad–about–you motto: Happy couples take bedroom breaks, which actually boost their love. Just because lust levels shift over time doesn't mean the hottest part of your relationship will be a cup of cocoa. The key to a deeply satisfying sex life is exploring all sides of each other, not just the physical, says Glass. When you spend out-of-bed hours together – cooking dinner, browsing in a shop, walking through the park – you're clicking on other levels and getting turned on by each other in new ways. Call it all-day mental foreplay.

When Rebecca, 28 enrolled in a wine-tasting course with her boyfriend, Paul, she gained much more than a sophisticated palate. 'Taking the train to the course was such as a turn on,' she says. 'Giggling together on the journey and growing passionate about oaky undertones was surprisingly exciting. I realise our sex life is sparked all day by little things we share, whether it's a private joke or a great bottle of Merlot.'

LOVE MYTH 2
Perfect couples miss each other whenever they're apart.
Reality check: Sentimental songs aside, it's the couples who don't crave an occasional split that usually career towards Splitsville. If you have identical experiences day after day, the line where he stops and you start begins to blur. 'A couple is made up of two

MAINTAINING YOUR OWN LIFE MAKES LUST LAST. SPENDING TIME ON YOUR OWN HELPS DEFINE WHO YOU ARE AND THE PERSON HE FELL IN LOVE WITH.

individuals,' says Myreah Moore, author of Date Like A Man To Get What You Want (HarperCollins). 'If you morph into each other, that leaves only one person. Eventually, the relationship becomes so bland and boring, it just peters out.'

Cosmo's mad–about–you motto: Maintaining your own life makes lust last. Spending time on your own is an opportunity to indulge in the hobbies and desires that define who you are and make you the passionate, diverse diva he fell in love with. 'My girlfriend is really into collecting records,' says Sam, 28. 'I love it when she introduces me to new music, but the biggest turn-on is that she knows everything about 80s music. It's exciting to see her so intense about something.'

'If you want a really electric connection, make a point of not seeing each other every night,' says Vogels. Schedule time to go out with friends or just do your own thing. You may find it hard to prise yourselves apart, but is there anything more passion-inducing than missing each other like mad?

LOVE MYTH 3
You can tell each other everything.
Reality check: They don't call it 'brutal' honesty for nothing. Even if your man says he's tough enough,

your confessions have the power to bruise his heart. 'When I first started dating Mark, I drank too much at a party one night and ended up kissing another man,' says Nancy, 26. 'I told Mark. Now that stupid kiss still haunts him four months later.'

Cosmo's mad–about–you motto: Every couple has a few skeletons in the closet. Think of the unique, totally yours union you'll build if you don't saddle your new relationship with old luggage. Everyone has a past, points out Judith Kuriansky, author of *The Complete Idiot's Guide To Dating* (Alpha Books), and those learning experiences prepared you both for this relationship. But confessing how great sex with your ex was will accomplish nothing.

How to know what to keep to yourself? 'Ask yourself whether you would want to hear this kind of information from him, says Vogels. 'If you have to share something sensitive because it effects your relationship, that's one thing. But if it's just some jealousy riling secret, just keep quiet.'

LOVE MYTH 4
Predictability is the death of passion.
Reality check: OK, nobody longs for a Groundhog Day romance, but

WRITE DOWN THE TEN QUALITIES THAT MOST MATTER TO YOU IN A MAN, THEN COUNT UP HOW MANY YOUR MAN HAS. HE SHOULD RATE AT LEAST A SIX.

we do need some degree of routine to relax into a comfort zone with our lover. 'There' a real intimacy in knowing each other's habits, likes, dislikes and reactions,' says Vogels. 'It's the way you form your own private club.'

Cosmo's mad–about–you motto: Rituals keep the relationship rolling. Those quirky (or not so quirky) customs are what make your relationship special. So instead of seeking out novelty for its own sake, celebrate everything that's unique to the two of you. 'Since we met last year, Eve and I have scheduled a weekly 70s TV night,' says Tom, 29. 'We both grew up loving *The Saint*, *The New Avengers* and *The Professionals*. It was one of the nostalgic things we laughed about on our first date, so watching the videos together reminds us how glad we are we've found each other.'

LOVE MYTH 5
If he loves you, he'll change.
Reality check: If he's not your dream man right now, don't expect him to transform into Mr Perfect. 'Our basic natures are formed by the time we're about five years old,' explains Glass. Spend your time focused on what might happen in the future and you'll miss all the good things occurring now.

Cosmo's mad–about–you motto: If you adore the very core of your man, any developments (or lack of) that hit you down the road won't be relationship wreckers. 'It's the surprising twists and turns of each partner's personal growth that keep a relationship from stagnating,' says Vogels.

Write down the ten qualities that matter most to you in a man – sense of humour, culinary skills, money. Then count up how many your man has. He should rate at least a six. If he comes up short, rather than trying to fix his 'flaws', check your list for any criteria you can live without. He has two left feet? See if you can survive without him on the dance floor. You might find it's even nicer to have him waiting for you on the sidelines while you take the spotlight.

LOVE MYTH 6
You have eyes only for each other.
Reality check: You're in love, not isolated on a deserted island. Attractive, engaging people cross your path every day, so it's inevitable you'll both be mildly tempted from time to time.
Cosmo's mad–about–you motto: Harmless crushes can fuel your fire for each other. 'Getting turned on by all sorts of people and situations

IF YOU WANT A REALLY ELECTRIC CONNECTION, MAKE A POINT OF NOT SEEING EACH OTHER EVERY NIGHT.

is a sign that you're healthy, red-blooded sexual beings,' says Vogels. We go even further and suggest that being sexually aware (which includes eyeing a cutey in his Calvins in an ad on the side of a bus) is a pre-requisite for a hot lust life with your partner.

This is confirmed by Phil, 27. 'I'm a barman, which my girlfriend used to consider a liability,' he says. 'But the truth is, being around that sex buzz all night. watching people drink, flirt and dance close, just makes me obsess about how fast I can get out of work and be with her.'

AND NOW, FOUR LOVE TRUTHS YOU CAN COUNT ON
If it's real, these smoochy scenarios should be part of the deal...

1 HE'LL LOVE YOU THROUGH THICK AND THIN
If it's true love, you can gain a stone, have a Joan of Arc fringe, lose your temper once in a while – and still have a relationship at the end of it. 'Real love is about being able to weather change even when life becomes stormy,' says Cherie Carter-Scott, author of If Love Is A Game, These Are The Rules (Vermilion). 'A solid romance means your man's turned on by who you are, warts, frizzy perm, and all.'

ADAM OLSZEWSKI

2 YOU ALWAYS HAVE SOMEONE TO FLIRT WITH

Just because you're a couple doesn't mean your flirting days are gone. 'You already know you have chemistry,' says Carter-Scott. 'Now's the fun part of finding ways to keep it bubbling.'

3 IN-LOVE COUPLES DO ARGUE, BUT THEY FIGHT FAIR

That means keeping to the issue at hand. When you row, expect him

to steer clear of irrelevant insults, bringing up ancient history, making you feel small or gloating if he 'wins'. And the same rules apply to you.

4 BEING IN LOVE MEANS YOU GET A DAILY EGO BOOST

You can bank on your partner's compliments when they're needed most. 'A steady supply of self-image supplements feeds your appreciation for each other,' says Carter-Scott. ∎

ANNE FOUGEDOIRE FERREZ

QUIZ

CAN YOU TRUST HIM?

Your man faithfully swears he won't sleep around and promises to guard your cash machine pin number with his life. Do you believe him? This revealing quiz will help you to find out whether you should take his word – or just take off.

1 After a stag night, you find a Polaroid of your man with a D-cup stripper sitting on his lap. You ask him if women were there. He immediately replies:

a 'Ummm… no. It was just us guys guzzling beer and playing poker.'
b 'Well, one woman jumped out of a cake, but I barely noticed her.'
c 'Oh, yeah! And you should've seen just what Bambi Boom Boom did with a banana.'

2 You ask him to take care of your canary while you're away. When you return, he breaks the news: Tweety is taking an eternal nap. What's his excuse?

a 'That bird was in a bad way before I was put in charge. It's not my fault.'
b 'I raced to the vet when I heard Tweety wheeze – I was too late [sniff].'
c 'I called my sister who's a vet. She said it didn't sound too serious, so I didn't do anything. I'm so sorry.'

3 You can't take it! You have to spill your best friend's deepest dirt: she's having a fling with her 16–year–old neighbour. What are the first words out of your man's mouth?

a 'Her secret is safe with me.'
b 'You've just made me an accessory to a crime. I'm obligated to turn her in.'
c 'Wait until I tell the guys that Miss Priss is getting bagged by the paperboy!'

4 You've already worked yourselves into a foreplay frenzy when – oops! – you realise you've forgotten to buy condoms. His reaction?

a 'Don't worry about it. I've got a condom in my coat pocket. I'm as careful as you are.'
b 'I won't pressure you to go bareback, even though I have just tested negative for every known STD. I'll just run out to the late-night chemist.'
c 'Don't worry, baby. I'll pull out in time.'

5 He wants to borrow your fresh–off–the–car–lot convertible to drive to his college reunion. To prove he's worthy to get behind the wheel, he:

a Offers to take a driving test – with you as the instructor. If he fails, no car.
b Swears that every single speeding ticket he's ever received has been a cruel miscarriage of justice.
c Tries his hardest to please you in bed, then asks 'Now can I have the car?'

6 His ex – whom you fondly refer to as 'that slut' – calls your man and asks him to dinner. When you tell him you're less than pleased, he:

a Rants about how he's totally over her – yet never says he won't go.
b Calls her right in front of you and tells her it's not a good idea.
c Asks you to go with him so that you can make absolutely certain that nothing of a naked nature goes on.

7 While making love, you reveal a secret sexual fantasy: being in bed with him and another man. What does he do with this red–hot info?

a Nothing, His policy is what goes on inside the bedroom stays in the bedroom.
b He gets drunk at a party and makes a lame joke about how your all-time favourite film is *Threesome*.
c He brags to his Neanderthal mate, who in turn informs you that he's 'ready for action' whenever you are.

8 You spot his car parked outside a bar known for its bikini–clad waitresses. He said he'd be watching the football at his friend's house. Later, you ask how he enjoyed the game. He replies:

a 'Bob's television isn't working, so we ended up going to a total dive bar where we knew the game would be on.'

b 'There's no place better than Bob's! I'll be going over there all season.'

c 'Bob wanted to go to the Bikini Bar, so we did. It was hard keeping my eyes on the screen but my team won.'

9 You're having a hair–pulling day at work. You call your man and tell him that you'd be eternally grateful if he would take care of dinner and rent a comedy video. He:

a Makes pasta and picks up an 80s teen flick – your number one guilty pleasure.

b Picks up a pepperoni pizza (his favourite) and *Monty Python and the Holy Grail* (also his favourite).

c Leaves a note on the fridge saying: 'I'm at Bob's. Don't wait up.'

10 You bring him home to meet your parents. The biggest bombshell that he drops over dinner is:

a During the drive over, you sang along to a Barry Manilow tune on the radio.

b You were pulled over for speeding and tried to get out of the ticket by flirting with the policeman.

c The last time you brought a guy home, you escaped to a motel for 'alone time'.

Love does not consist in gazing at each other but in looking outward together in the same direction.

Antoine de Saint Exupéry

ERIC MCNATT

SCORING

1	a-0	b-1	c-2
2	a-0	b-2	c-1
3	a-2	b-1	c-0
4	a-2	b-1	c-0
5	a-2	b-1	c-0
6	a-0	b-2	c-1
7	a-2	b-1	c-0
8	a-1	b-0	c-2
9	a-2	b-1	c-0
10	a-2	b-1	c-0

16 POINTS OR MORE
Honest Beyond Belief

This winner would never intentionally let you down – but if he did, you can be sure he'd be the first to 'fess up about it. 'When he makes a promise, he does everything in his power to make it a reality,' says Mira Kirshenbaum, couples therapist and author of Our Love Is Too Good to Feel So Bad (Avon Books). 'And he's mature enough not to put a spin on things.'

That said, this nothing-to-hide policy can be a bit unsettling at times. After all, you really didn't need to know what Bambi Boom Boom did with that banana, now did you? And if his uncensored honesty is insensitive on a consistent basis, there's a chance he may be using the truth as an underhanded way to be hurtful. If that's the case, give the candid cad the kiss-off. But if he's just a straight shooter, don't be afraid to let him aim right at your heart.

8 TO 15 POINTS
He's Only Human

When he says he's going to do something, you can usually count on it. However, there are sometimes situations when his actions don't match his words. 'Even good guys go back on their promises to protect their own interests,'explains David J Lieberman, author of Never Be Lied to Again (St Martin's Press). 'When he lies about a specific touchy issue, he's doing it because that's what he thinks you want to hear.'

Just as long as he never sets out to upset you and keeps confidences when it really counts, this guy is definitely a keeper. And as the relationship deepens, he'll realise he doesn't need those little white lies to keep love alive.

7 POINTS OR FEWER
Let–You–Down Loser

Face facts: if your guy has a history of sketchy behaviour – he constantly blames others for his screw-ups and always makes you a million empty promises – he's destined to let you down. Even if the guy means no harm, his behaviour is bound to put you in a chronic state of frustration and fear. 'You will never trust what he says and you won't be able to trust your own judgement about him either,' says Kirshenbaum.

Ask yourself why you're putting up with the get-set-to-be-let-down cycle. You may have bad-boy blinkers on – you desperately want the relationship to work, so you conveniently overlook all the inconsistencies. 'But wishful thinking cannot allow you to lose sight of reality,' says Lieberman. So if you find you are repeatedly let down by your irresponsible man, move on – or you'll never be able to separate fiction from fact and get the devotion you totally deserve.

ANNA PALMA

HOW TO SPOT A LIAR

Have a sinking feeling that your man isn't on the level? Here's how to tell if he's just feeding you a load of BS.

HIS BODY BETRAYS HIM

Avoiding physical contact isn't the only clue that his word isn't worth squat. 'If he clasps his hands tightly or stuffs them in his pockets, he's really saying "I'm keeping something inside",' says David Lieberman, a body-language expert. Also, watch out if his hands go up to his face or neck when he's talking, which is an unconscious attempt to distract and hide his lies. Half-hearted gestures – like lazy shrugs and weak smiles – also convey lack of conviction.

HE SHUTS UP ASAP

If you suspect he's lying, don't make accusations – just ask innocent-sounding questions. A guilty man will always rush to end the conversation. 'He knows the longer the interrogation lasts, the greater his chances of being caught

out,' says Lieberman. Truth-tellers, on the other hand, speak with complete ease, simply because they have nothing to hide.

HE OVERLOOKS YOUR LIE

Try this simple sincerity test: when he's right in the middle of his spiel, roll in a little fib of your own. 'When he's telling you about the bar he went to with the guys, mention that you heard there was a major fire in that road at the same time,' offers Lieberman. If he's bogus, he'll either ignore your comment or give fake details to corroborate his story. But if he's telling you the truth, he'll make a point of saying he saw nary a fire engine or puff of smoke – just to prove you wrong. ■

Only little boys and old men sneer at love.

Louis Auchincloss

Never forget that the most powerful force on earth is love.

Nelson Rockefeller

THE MOST *Romantic* THING THAT EVER HAPPENED TO ME

ERIC MCNATT

■ One winter night, I got a craving for chocolate. There wasn't any in the flat. An hour later my boyfriend called me up to the bedroom. He was under the duvet, naked with two unwrapped KitKats! He'd snuck out into the cold to satisfy my craving.
Katie, 28, GP

■ During that awkward getting-to-know-you stage he told me, 'Pack an overnight bag and be ready to leave tomorrow after work. No questions.' There was so much mystery, I could hardly sleep. The next evening, we drove and drove but I still had no idea where we were heading. There was a snowstorm on the way. At dusk, we pulled up to the most picture-perfect little log cabin. He lit a fire and cooked for me. It was a prelude to an unforgettable night.
Angela, 33, architect

■ It all happened on Valentine's Day. I work in an office full of women and I'd briefed my boyfriend on the importance of receiving flowers. But, horror of horrors, by 2pm everyone else was showing off their spoils, and I hadn't received so much as a daisy. Then the delivery man staggered through the door carrying a massive bouquet of deep red roses – yes! – for me! I opened the note and it said, 'Marry me.' Was he joking? I read it five more times, then rang him and said, 'I say yes!' He said 'You're sure? Thanks!' When I got home that evening, the whole flat was decorated with pink and red hearts. He'd taken the afternoon off, bought coloured paper and spent hours cutting out heart shapes, He'd put champagne on ice, made dinner and lit candles, Then, he got on one knee and proposed again because he 'wasn't there when it happened the first time'.
Anne, 26, writer

■ We'd just met and went out to dinner. I was nervous and drank too much too quickly. I went to the loo and, as I touched up my mascara, I knocked my contact lens out. Staggering around in a boozy panic, I stepped back and heard the lens break under my high heels. I'm so short-sighted, I barely made it back to the table. I had to put a hand over my eye to focus each time I put food on my fork! I was so embarrassed, but he was so sweet. I looked utterly ridiculous, but he treated me as if I was the most beautiful, elegant woman in the world. Through my myopic haze, I could see I'd found the man who'd make my life complete.
Olivia, 26, PA

■ I was walking through town when I accidentally stepped off a curb in front of a bicycle courier. He had to brake suddenly but, instead of shouting at me, he smiled this beautiful smile and motioned me to keep walking. I shouted 'Thank you' and he slowly rode off, looking at me. Several streets later, we passed each other again. He looked me in the eyes and said 'You're so beautiful! I have to know your name.' I spluttered it out. He stared at me as if I was a goddess, then rode off.
Jenny, 22, photographer

■ I was facing a frighteningly hectic week, I told a prospective Romeo one Sunday. He said he'd hardly anything to do. 'I'll come and be your slave,' he said. I jokingly told him I'd get him doing what our work experience people do: trot out to Dunkin' Donuts to buy me a large weak tea. On Monday morning, a package arrived in the office for me, containing a large weak tea and a bag full of baby doughnuts. Tuesday brought tea and a large bunch of sweet grapes; Wednesday, tea in a funny mug; Thursday, more tea and a beautiful bouquet of flowers. On Friday, the man himself turned up to ask me out. How could I possibly refuse?
Naomi, 29, banker

■ I once had a very passionate affair with a DJ. The day after our first date – when he'd professed undying love – I was utterly distraught because he hadn't called. I turned on the radio and tuned into his station just to hear his voice. He put on *Last Night A DJ Saved My Life*, then went on speaking to me in coded messages! It would have meant nothing out-of-the-ordinary to the listener, but it was so significant to us. We were having a love affair on national radio! It was public and intimate, and it turned me to jelly.
Mary, 24, psychologist

■ My boyfriend Ian works in this place full of lads. One night, a macho colleague said, 'Where are you off to?' Ian said, 'To see Kim.' The man (he didn't like me) said, 'You still going with her?' Ian said, in front this man and his tough friends, 'Yes. And she's beautiful and I love her very much and I'm going to marry her!' He never told me, but a friend of mine overheard and blabbed!
Kim, 28, designer

■ We were going to a party, and I was at my boyfriend's house. He was being really slow getting ready, and I was getting angrier and angrier. We were an hour late, and he was still faffing about in the bathroom. Then I heard a beeping noise upstairs. It was the electric organiser I'd bought him as a present. 'Can you sort that out?' he shouted through the bathroom door. I stomped upstairs, fuming. The organiser was on his bed. I felt like throwing it out the window. I picked it up and looked at the message. It said, 'Marry me?' I screamed, then charged into the bathroom, where I found an all-dressed-up-and-ready-to-go boyfriend sitting on the floor, diamond ring in hand. OK, so he didn't know how to set the time on his organiser but I still said yes!
Rebecca, 27, lawyer ■

TAMARA SCHLESINGER

I don't want to live –
I want to love first
and live incidentally.

Zelda Fitzgerald

BUTCH HOGAN

DO YOU MAKE YOUR LOVER
feel loved?

A man reveals why simply saying
'I love you!' isn't enough to make him
feel truly cherished.

IF YOU LOVE HIM, YOU WANT HIM TO FEEL THE WARMTH AND DEPTH OF YOUR LOVE, JUST AS HE WANTS TO MAKE YOU FEEL CHERISHED.

F eeling loved is one of the most powerful needs known to man or woman, right up there with sex, shelter and a reliable supply of chocolate. Everyone needs to feel loved. Happy relationships depend on it. And if you love him, you want him to feel the warmth and depth of your love – just as he wants to make you feel cherished.

But knowing what it takes to make your lover feel loved isn't always easy. Too much attention, and you're smothering him. Too many presents, and he feels he's being emotionally blackmailed. Too many insistent 'I love you's and he could feel as though you're browbeating him into a response when all he really wants to do at that moment is to relax peacefully on the sofa and watch the semi-final of the European Cup, with you by his side.

You may feel you're sending out the signals, but the question is, does he receive them the right way? Or at all? Does he feel starved of love by a partner too cold to show what she really feels? Or bombarded with it by an emotional time bomb? What you're lacking here is vital information from the person who's on the receiving end of these signals.

That can all be remedied, according to psychologist Philip Rogers, author of *Do You Feel Loved By Me?* (Living Well Publications). 'We put great emphasis on the words involved with love, and particularly the words "I love you",' he says. 'But why do we so rarely ask, "Do you feel loved by me?" When you love someone, isn't it more important they feel truly loved, rather than you feeling you love them?'

By asking the potentially scary question, 'Do you feel loved by me?', you're opening the doors to a two-way flow of information with your partner. If that seems too frightening, try asking 'When do you feel most loved by me? What could I say or do that would make you feel really loved?' The vital thing here is that you must be open-minded and accepting when you ask these questions – your man may well not give you the answer you expect! The whole point of this is to discover more about your relationship and deepen intimacy. Says Rogers, 'It can be very helpful if a man can share his experience of being loved with you. Because then you are talking honestly with each other and not relying on assumptions and mind-reading which can lead you into all sorts of trouble.'

Understanding that emotional fulfilment, just like sexual fulfilment, depends on constant feedback, is a big step, and it's probably not one he'll find easy, After all, most men don't exactly have a great track record when it comes to discussing relationships in a free and frank manner. The words 'blood' and 'stone' spring to mind, in fact. But that doesn't mean he

won't respond if you take the lead – non-verbally. Try some of the make-his-heart-flip ideas here; see how he reacts to them. But never forget feeling loved is something he needs, and it will reap enormous benefits for you, too. Figure out how to do it, and you might just secure a hold on his heart even welding equipment won't shift.

LOVE STRATEGY *1*

Say it when you mean it

In the early stages of a relationship, much time and emotional energy is spent finding out what's going on in your partner's head. Does he love me? Is he playing games? Will he hate my mother? The first 'I love you's are a defining moment in this process, like a transaction finally made after a lot of horse-trading. The trouble is that later on that transaction can become as mechanical as a direct debit.

According to Philip Rogers, 'It's sad to say, but someone may use the words "I love you" and it can be a lie or said out of duty or habit. "I love you" can be arrogant, used to claim something – like ownership. It can be said expecting a similar declaration in return.'

Try rationing the three little words, suggests Will, 32, a fund manager at a London bank. 'I used

*L*OVE NOTE

MAKE SMALL TALK – TRY CHATTING EACH OTHER UP, EVEN IF YOU HAVE BEEN TOGETHER FOR AGES.

NOEL J.FEDERIZO

to hate the whole "love you", "love you back" parroting thing,' he says. 'Although, of course, I've been as guilty of it as anyone.' His girlfriend, Julie, was different from the start. 'It took her a long time to say it. She said it because she meant it, and she saves it for moments when it really counts. Like after Sunday lunch, when we're walking along the river together, there might be a

SAVE THOSE THREE LITTLE WORDS FOR THE MOMENTS WHEN THEY WILL REALLY COUNT.

moment when she slips her arm through mine and whispers in my ear, "I love you so much". It makes me feel like I own the world.'

Other words count, too. 'I love being told by my partner that she finds me attractive or that I look good in what I'm wearing.' says TV researcher Jasper, 29, 'I think women forget it's a thing men never hear, except from a lover.

LOVE STRATEGY *2*

Put your hands on him

Men like being touched; they live a pretty touch-free life – unless they play rugby. You're probably the only person who gives him any tender, physical attention. Andy, a 32-year-old manager, likes being manhandled by his girlfriend: 'It starts with her looking for my door keys when we've come back from shopping and I'm loaded with bags. Instead of asking for them, she delves into my pockets. It's sexy, makes me laugh and I feel very close to her.'

LOVE STRATEGY *3*

Give him elbow room

Letting a man have the space to do the things he wants to do is one of the most grown-up ways of making him feel loved. 'I think it's really important,' says Rob, 27, a market researcher. 'I need to feel I can do some things my girlfriend wouldn't enjoy – watch a football match at a friend's house, see a thrash band or watch a John Woo movie – without feeling either guilty about it, or, worse, feeling obliged to take her along and spoil it for both of us.'

ANNA PALMA

Paul, 28, an ad agency media buyer, agrees. 'My girlfriend and I have a lot of things in common, but football isn't one of them. She's completely uninterested in it, but I'm a keen Everton fan. Then one week out of the blue, she bought a pair of Everton tickets as a present, for me and a friend. I was gobsmacked – my mouth didn't work. It was her way of saying, go and enjoy it. I don't mind – in fact, I want you to. I think understandings like that strengthen ties rather than weaken them.'

LOVE STRATEGY *4*
Remember the little things

The longer any relationship goes on, the easier it becomes to forget those little things that drove you crazy with desire at the beginning. 'Like making eyes at each other across a crowded dinner party,' explains Tom, 27, a film writer. 'I'll be in the middle of telling a story, or a joke, or just talking to someone, and I'm suddenly aware that Rose is watching me from somewhere down the table with these incredibly gooey eyes. I love the incidentalness of it. It's not a big declaration, it's just a moment, but that's what makes it so great.'

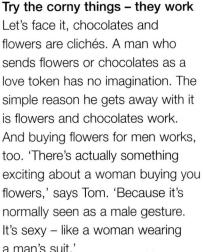

*L*OVE NOTE
LEAVE THE PARTY EARLY. ACCORDING TO RESEARCH, THE MOST POPULAR TIME TO MAKE LOVE IS 10.34PM.

LOVE STRATEGY *5*
Try the corny things – they work

Let's face it, chocolates and flowers are clichés. A man who sends flowers or chocolates as a love token has no imagination. The simple reason he gets away with it is flowers and chocolates work. And buying flowers for men works, too. 'There's actually something exciting about a woman buying you flowers,' says Tom. 'Because it's normally seen as a male gesture. It's sexy – like a woman wearing a man's suit.'

Gary, 30, remembers a time when he'd had a hard few weeks at work when his project was rejected by an important client. 'My girlfriend sent me flowers to cheer me up. And they weren't roses, they were sort of manly flowers with lots of green and spiky things. Very stylish and so carefully chosen. The combination of thinking of me when I was down, and taking such care blew me away.' My colleagues were amazed – none of their girlfriends had ever done anything like it.'

LOVE STRATEGY *6*
Send him a message

Small messages, little gestures of love mean a lot. You think he'll find them soppy? Don't you believe it.

Keith, 31, an advertising art director, had a partner who put little chocolate hearts into his luggage when he went on film shoots. 'I'd find them when I was looking for clean socks,' he says. 'They'd have little messages – "I miss you", "Please hurry home", things like that. I found it incredibly touching.'

Small gifts work in the same way, especially if it's something he's talked about: a book, a CD maybe. It's not that you've spent money on him, it's that you've listened and taken time. 'I was going to Switzerland on business,' says Ben, 29, a systems analyst. 'I opened my bag at the airport and found a copy of a book I'd wanted a few months before but hadn't been able to find. My girlfriend had ordered it specially. What struck me most was she'd gone to the trouble of doing it. Of course, I know she cares about me. But at that moment, I really felt it.'

The internet has opened a whole new world of possibilities for the electronic billet-doux. There's something both immediate and detached about the technology that encourages lovers to be more uninhibited than they might otherwise be. As Mark, a 30-year-old graphic designer, discovered when he first surfed the internet at work. 'The first thing I saw was a message from my girlfriend. It said, 'I'm glad you're on the internet. Now I can tell you how much I want to shag your brains out tonight.' It was quite out of character for her, but I loved it.' You can even send him virtual flowers via the internet. Contact www.virtualflorist.com to choose anything from a single stem rose to a bunch of daffs.

LOVE STRATEGY 7

Let him be weak sometimes

Most of the time, men feel under fantastic pressure to be manly, to be strong, in control, tough. If you and your lover are walking down a deserted street in a dodgy part of town late at night, only one of you has permission to be scared – and it's not him. A woman who is terrified to see her man cry or be afraid can never really be intimate with him. So one of the greatest gifts a woman can give a man is to let him be weak or silly – and still love and admire him.

'One of the times I feel most loved is when my girlfriend uses her very silly pet name for me – which I certainly couldn't tell anyone else,' says Tim, 30. 'It's so secret and intimate – it's just for me and it binds us into a special circle of

ℒOVE NOTE
WRITE AN EROTIC LETTER AND HIDE IT IN HIS BRIEFCASE BEFORE SENDING HIM OFF TO WORK.

ANNA PALMA

two. It's like she sees a vulnerable side of me nobody else does, but she still really loves me. It makes me feel accepted.'

LOVE STRATEGY 8

Be there when he needs you

There are times in life when the chips are down and feeling loved may be just about the only thing he has to hold on to. Melodramatic? It happened to James, then a 22-year-old, fresh out of college. He'd had major surgery and was in hospital on heavy medication.

'My father was out of the country at the time, my mother was an alcoholic and my brother was too wrapped up in his career to help,' he says. 'Kate was the one who came, every day, to my bedside. She was the one who saw me through.' Ten years later, they're still together, now with two children. 'Feeling loved like that is a kind of investment,' adds James. 'You draw on it in the years afterwards.' ■

I feel the earth move under my feet
I feel the sky tumbling down
I feel my heart start
a-trembling
Whenever you're around.

Carole King

ANNA PALMA

IS YOUR RELATIONSHIP OVERDRAWN?

Consider this quiz an emotional bank statement and check out the true state of your relationship. Are you brave enough to give truly honest answers?

We've all been as sweet as Candarel to the waiter and as grizzly as a old bear to our lover. If it's a special occasion – he forgot your birthday, or laughed at your efforts on the dance floor – such behaviour is excusable. But sometimes, we deny our partners vital love and affection.

Sandra Scantling, author of *Extraordinary Sex Now*

(Doubleday), likens a relationship to a bank account. Every snide remark or sour glance is a hefty withdrawal, every compliment or gentle touch a big fat cheque. 'Make loving, appreciative deposits regularly and your investments will magnify. But all too often we stop making deposits. And before we know it, we're overdrawn,' she says.

1 You're getting ready to go out together. Pick the line you're most likely to say:

a 'Turn off the TV *now*. I hate it when we're late.'
b 'Mmm, you smell nice.'
c 'You're not going out wearing that are you?'

2 The last time you left him a note, it read something like:

a 'Your mother rang. Kept me on the phone for three hours, so watch out.'
b 'I adore you, my darling! PS: shall we do it later?'
c 'Bring home milk.'

3 A £387.14 phone bill arrives. Your partner pleads poverty and asks you to pay this one. You say:

a 'Pardon me, but how much did that new stereo of yours cost again?'
b 'Hmm Maybe I should stop calling Sarah in New York for long chats every weekend.'
c 'Oh, why not, seeing as I already pay for every single bill anyway.'

4 He used to buy you flowers. You love being bought flowers. Now, flowers are as scarce as footballers with degrees.

a You say, 'I'd like you to buy me flowers more. And make sure they're sent via the office.'
b You buy him flowers. You buy yourself flowers. You hope he'll get the idea.
c You say, 'Claire's boyfriend sent her this amazing bouquet. He's such a sweetie.'

5 Your partner is flouncing around like Julian Clary on a bad hair day. Your most likely response is:

a 'Ooh temper, temper!'
b 'What's up?'
c 'Snap out of it, you're acting like a five-year-old.'

6 He's putting on weight and shows no inclination to drink less beer and/or walk anywhere. If you dropped a hint, it would be:

a 'Why don't you come to aerobics with me this week? Lots of men do it.'
a 'I want to go on a health kick. Will you help me?'
c 'I really don't think you need that pudding.'

7 His birthday is imminent. He's been dropping hints about how much his life would be enhanced by the latest computer gizmo. You've already bought a present. What do you do?

a His wish is your command! You rush to the shops, agonise over which gadget to buy, and know you'll make his day.
b Yours is not to reason why. You duly nip down to Dixons, fork out the cash, give it to him early and still give him your original present.
c Sod the computer – treating him to a night at the ballet is infinitely more romantic.

8 Your partner arrives at home unexpectedly. He's distraught

because he's lost his job. Your gut reaction:

a You hug him and say 'But that's impossible! I don't believe it!'
b You hug him and say 'It's alright. We'll sort this.'
c You stare and say 'But that's impossible! You must have done something. What was it?'

9 You're mid–passion when, shock horror, his manhood wilts. He says he's tired and offers you oral sex to compensate. You say:

a 'Alright, but let's try and do it properly afterwards.'
b 'Actually, I feel in the mood just to cuddle.'
c 'Oh, forget it. I wasn't really into it anyway.'

10 He brings you a cup of coffee in bed on Saturday morning. You thank him and drink it. Then you say,

a 'Where's the toast, boy?'
b 'Your thank-you gift is under the covers.'
c 'Actually, that coffee was too weak for me.'

SCORING

MOSTLY As

In credit – just

Your relationship isn't in the red – yet – but it certainly isn't in the pink. Because at present, it's all about you. You pleasantly, but very firmly, ignore his wants, feelings, needs. Do you subconsciously resent him because he's so self-centred – or is it actually your fault?

MOSTLY Bs

You're an emotional millionaire

In your house, Bill Gates is referred to as 'the pauper'. You are so supportive that Marks & Spencer could sell you in their lingerie department and make a mint. We trust your man is equally rich in charm, love, humour, and affection. If not, he should be. You deserve it.

RAFAL ZABIK

Red, red whine

Wow! You're so in the red you could wear your bank balance to a party – not! He must have committed a heinous crime to deserve such unfeeling treatment. Oh, and emotionally speaking, you owe the gross national debt of Bolivia. Better start saving…

SIX STEPS TO PUSH YOU BACK INTO THE BLACK

1 RECOGNISE THE SIGNS OF POVERTY

Resentment, frustration, bad temper, bad hearing… 'You stop caring how the other person feels,' says relationship psychologist Dr Valerie Lamont. 'You may be sarcastic and unwilling to empathise.'

2 PINPOINT THE CAUSE OF YOUR OVERDRAFT

Face it. Loverboy bears the brunt if your job is overly irksome. Don't stomp around at home, find the root of the issue and speak to your boss or take time off – don't take it out on him.

3 HAVE A CONFERENCE

If your overdraft stems from you playing the martyr – and minding – speak up. 'Don't wait for resentment to build up, talk about it at the first hint: "You promised you'd put petrol in the car, but you didn't. Is there anything wrong?" You can be affectionate rather than accusatory,' suggests Dr Julia Cole, psychosexual therapist and Relate counsellor.

4 ASK HIM TO SUGGEST A SAVING STRATEGY

If your partner is so deep in the red he's scarlet – and with no palpable excuse, Dr Lamont suggests 'Talking about some of the things he used to do for you: say "Remember how you used to bring me breakfast in bed?" Tell him how good that made you feel.'

5 DON'T FORCE EACH OTHER INTO BAD INVESTMENTS

You think you're loving because you took him to see *The Nutcracker* on his birthday. All he wanted was a Swiss army knife. That's not taking care of his needs. It's taking care of yours. 'A good relationship is matching what you do with what they want,' says Dr Lamont.

6 START SAVING THE PENNIES

And this one takes humility. Dr Scantling advises, 'If you have to criticise, have three appreciation comments for every criticism. It sounds orchestrated, but it's what makes a good relationship.' And make a big deposit from time to time. 'For one evening a week, treat each other like guests,' says Scantling. 'Light candles, open a bottle of wine… and give him 100 per cent of your attention.' ∎

Had we never lov'd sae kindly,
Had we never lov'd sae blindly,
Never met – or never parted
We had ne'er been broken-hearted.

Robert Burns

JUST £1.50
a copy

when you subscribe to **Cosmopolitan** for **just £4.49** by quarterly direct debit

For glamorous fashion and beauty, ground-breaking features and the latest health and careers news, treat yourself to a subscription to Cosmopolitan and **SAVE 46%** on the full rate!

Subscribers enjoy:

- **JUST £1.50** a copy (usual price £2.80)
- **SAVE OVER** £15 a year
- **FREE** home delivery
- **Just £4.49** by quarterly direct debit

HURRY! This offer is strictly limited!

Cosmopolitan – PRIORITY SUBSCRIPTION ORDER FORM

Your details   Ref: XA04

Please complete in block capitals.

❏ Yes, I would like to subscribe to *Cosmopolitan*.

Ms/Miss/Mrs/Mr_____Initials_____
Surname _____
Address _____
_____Postcode_____
Date of birth_____
Home telephone number_____
Mobile telephone number_____
Email_____

Please tick this box if you would like to receive information and offers from The National Magazine Company Ltd by: email ❏ SMS ❏
Please tick this box if you would like to receive information and offers from selected companies by: email ❏ SMS ❏

Gift subscription   Ref: XA04

(Please fill in your details above when giving as a gift.)

❏ Please send *Cosmopolitan* as a gift to the person below.

Ms/Miss/Mrs/Mr_____Initials_____
Surname _____
Address _____
_____Postcode_____

DIRECT Debit
The National Magazine Co. Ltd

Originator's ID number
820407   **£4.49 per quarter**

To the manager (Bank name) _____
Address _____
_____Postcode_____
Name(s) of account holder(s) _____

Branch sort code ⬚⬚ ⬚⬚ ⬚⬚

Bank/Building Society account number ⬚⬚⬚⬚⬚⬚⬚⬚

Ref No. (for National Magazine Co Ltd use only) ⬚⬚⬚⬚⬚

INSTRUCTION TO YOUR BANK OR BUILDING SOCIETY TO PAY BY DIRECT DEBIT
Please pay The National Magazine Company Ltd Direct Debits from the account detailed in this instruction, subject to the safeguards assured by The Direct Debit Guarantee. I understand that this instruction may remain with The National Magazine Co Ltd and, if so, details may be passed electronically to my Bank/Building Society.

Signature(s)_____Date_____
Banks and Building Societies may not accept Direct Debit instructions for some types of account.

SIMPLY SEND THIS COUPON TO:

FREEPOST MID21595, MARKET HARBOROUGH, LE16 7BR

This offer is valid for UK subscriptions only, and is available when paying by quarterly direct debit. All orders will be acknowledged and advised of commencement issue within 14 days. This offer cannot be used in conjunction with any other subscription offer and closes 31 May 2004. The full UK subscription rate is £33.60. All information is correct at time of going to press. For subscription enquiries, call 01858 438838. The National Magazine Company Ltd may use your details to let you know about other products and services that we think would be of interest to you. Please tick here if you prefer not to receive any information from The National Magazine Company Ltd ❏. Occasionally, we may also pass your details to selected companies. If you do not wish to receive their products or offers, please tick this box ❏. The National Magazine Company Ltd is registered as a data controller under the Data Protection Act 1998. The National Magazine Company Ltd, 72 Broadwick Street, London W1F 9EP.

You can order by calling our hotline on: **01858 438844**   Quote ref: XA04
Open weekdays 8am to 9.30pm; Saturdays 8am to 4pm

You can also order securely online. Simply visit **www.subscription.co.uk/cosmo** and quote: **XA04**